STEPPING OUT
THE THRILL OF
TRAVELLING

STEPPING OUT
THE THRILL OF
TRAVELLING

by

Sean Jenkins

British Library Cataloguing in Publication Data A catalogue record for this
book is available from the British Library

ISBN: 978-1-291-40170-7

Produced in association with
Biographies & Memoirs
Springfield, Lower Kingsdown Road, Kingsdown, Corsham, Wilts SN13 8BA
www.biographiesandmemoirs.co.uk
Typeset in Goudy Old Style by www.wordsbydesign.co.uk

This book is dedicated to all my family.

Mum, Dad, Allison, Ian, Harry and Jamie,
and to my soul mate Trudy.
I love you all!

A big mention must also go to all the friends I've partied
with over the years at sea and on land – it's been a great laugh
and a fantastic journey.

I would also like to thank Judi Cuervo, a travel writer
friend of mine from New York. She both inspired me and
encouraged me to never give up on my ambition to see my
own travels in print. I hope you're still enjoying your Cosmos?

Contents

To Seb

Happy Readings!
Go see the world

A Word from the Author

Dear Readers,

I've always wanted to write something about my life and the travelling I have done, enjoying all the experiences of the world and all its sights and sounds.

I'd like to think I've had an interesting lifestyle through my teens, twenties and thirties doing more than the average person. This is in no way disrespecting the lifestyles other people like friends and family chose.

This is a book about my experiences and a celebration of my life to date. I hope you will get as much enjoyment out of reading them as I did out of experiencing them. Now I've reached 46 and I have all these years of travelling behind me I often get asked the question, 'So where have you been then Sean?'

The easiest way to answer the inquisitive one is by the now-familiar, 'There aren't many places that I haven't been to.' The one question that always stumps me though is: 'So which is your favourite?' In a polite way I hate this question because the interrogator wants me to commit myself to a kind of 'and the winner is' situation.

The world is full of so many beautiful places I defy anybody to answer that question successfully - I bet even Judith Chalmers would struggle with that one! How can anyone define their favourite place? Do you look at its natural beauty or stand in awe at its modern architecture, maybe you stroll amongst its tranquil settings or enjoy the hustle and bustle of its city living? Every place is different and you enjoy them all for different reasons. It's a really difficult answer to give to a really difficult question.

This book is something I wanted to have as a personal chronicle of my life to show my two nephews Harry and Jamie so that it inspires them and hopefully others to travel and see everything the world has to offer. Instead of accepting what life gives you when you're young and you've just left school, go out and find and enjoy what life has for you.

Life is such much more fun when you find it for yourself. Along the way you will view some of my favourite photographs from my own personal collection which I regard as my pride and joy.

The hardest task that I came across was actually choosing which cities and stories I wanted to put into the book, because of course there are some that you don't really want to know about (he says with a cheeky smirk on his face). So I've saved you the embarrassment and just picked the interesting ones – okay.

My first travelling experiences, like every other kid, started in the back of my dad's car. Some weekends in the summer he would take us somewhere up and down the northern coastline (weather permitting of course, this is England I'm talking about), only to get there when my sister and I would start fighting, so Dad would cut the trip short for punishment.

Getting a wee bit older I then ventured onto the National Express buses (England's answer to the Greyhound buses). I would love taking long trips, sat there with my Walkman (pre-CD player and iPod times), and staying a couple of days with friends. It wasn't long after that I took to the rail tracks but time and time again I would find myself on the wrong platform only to see ahead of me the train I should 'ave been on, pulling out of the station. And on the odd occasion I would find myself on the wrong train going in the opposite direction, most notably resulting in spending an evening sleeping rough at Bristol Temple Meads station with a girlfriend because we got onto the wrong train from London – but then the amount of alcohol we consumed might have had something to do with that.

My first trip on an aeroplane was a short trip across the water to Dublin, Ireland – I thought it was fantastic. Even today, though I've landed and taken off from every major airport and flown with every airline company, the whole scenario surrounding a long haul or short flight still gives me excited butterflies in my stomach.

'Is this guy crazy or what?' I can hear you nervous flyers ranting. It's so peaceful and hassle-free up there, knowing that these huge, fantastic flying machines were designed by those magnificent men for taking you to these faraway places of your dreams, places that you first learnt about during those geography lessons in school. It still gives me a kick of enjoyment.

Moving on from there I was introduced to a friend of a friend who had just completed his first contract at sea on board a cruise liner. My imagination was sailing away with me as I was sitting there in amazement at his stories of all the places he'd seen and the beaches he'd sat on with his girlfriends of different nationality. The great thing about this was that he was getting paid for it. The money sounded good but the destinations sounded better. This was a perfect way of seeing the world.

''Tis a ship's life for me... ha ha,' I say in my best Captain Jack's voice-over. And y'know what, the most ironic thing is that when I was a youngster going to and from school, one of my favourite places to play was a playground area that had a big iron framework of an old ship, right out of the novels of Sinbad. I would spend hours climbing to the crow's nest then to the bow and then the stern, keeping a look out for those nasty pirates or undiscovered land. If ever I was late home for my tea, casting off with that ship was always to blame. I had good times there in my innocent youth. I think the old ship is still there today!

I come from a divorced background and I would like to take this opportunity to put the minds of my mother and father to rest. Over the years they have often wondered why I was always away travelling, living like the nomad of the family. They have both asked me on separate occasions if their divorce was the reason for it. So I want to take this opportunity, in print with hand on heart —Mum and Dad, no it wasn't.

I did it because I wanted to, the family circumstances didn't force me. In fact I'd like to say thank you both for putting up with me and supporting me over the years. It was nice to know that you realised what my dreams were and what the things I wanted to do were so you both just let me get on with them.

My sister Allison has also played her part in encouraging me and my love for Harry and Jamie has inspired me to write this book, so thanks to you and Ian, for bringing them into all our lives.

I would also like to thank U2 for providing the music and lyrics along the way. They have been big influences on my life and have travelled everywhere with me.

And I would also like to be humble enough, while grinding my teeth, to say a small thank you to my ex-wife Casey for encouraging and pushing me to put pen to paper. Having the idea is one thing, to actually do it is another, so at least the robbing cow came in useful for something!

And not forgetting my long-supportive girlfriend, Trudy, who noticed the advert in the local community magazine pointing me in the direction of Wendy Cooper, who helped in the production of this book. Trudy, love ya lots babe x.

I think it's great that after all these years, here I am having just compiled my favourite memories of my life at sea in the shape of a book, that my young nephew Harry is getting inquisitive about the world and all its beauty. To quote a line from a favourite movie of mine:

The world is your oyster.

Love to you all, please enjoy x.

PS. I would also like to dedicate this book to all my old shipmates past and present, home or abroad. R.I.P. to those who have already joined the big crew party on the bridge of heavens ocean liner, I had great times with you all x.

One
Stepping Out – The Thrill of Travelling

Ever since I was a young kid, growing up in the harsh life and environment of the North East, I always dreamt of seeing the world and travelling. My friends at school had a totally different view of their lives ahead of them. They grew up to accept life as it was given to them. All of them had these ideas that it was normal to get a dead-end job, or even go straight on to the dole queue to receive hand-outs. A lot of them came from families with no sense of exploration. I guess when they were young it wasn't one of those 'in things'. Problem was though, they would never seem to encourage us to make better lives for ourselves or broaden our horizons, so we wouldn't think any different. Come the time we were old enough to leave school most of my school mates would be dreaming of becoming a member of the local social club (just because their dads were), getting their girlfriends pregnant, and settling down in a run-down council house. That was it – their whole life settled from an early age with huge life-changing responsibilities. Not for me!

I know everyone is different and I respect that, but have a little imagination. I can remember quite clearly looking at the trees outside my classroom window and seeing palm trees, going to the seaside with my family and seeing white sands and clear blue water instead of the rubbish-filled grey sand and murky freezing water!

It was clear to me I saw life in front of me very differently to them.

I first got the travelling bug when I was about 15-years-old and a keen boxer down at my local boxing club. When I was good enough to start fighting competition bouts, that's when it entered my blood. Week after week myself and the other guys from the gym, along with our coach would cram into the back of cars and travel up and down England – Liverpool, Hull, Coventry, Bristol, Cardiff and somewhere in Scotland. On one occasion I represented England in Denmark (robbed on points though).

The whole thrill of counting down the days then packing a sports bag, saying 'Goodbye' or 'See you later' to family and friends, then climbing in to the car or the occasional mini-bus, meeting different people everywhere. I would not change those memories for gold nor money – that sense of bonding and camaraderie is something that I loved and would experience again in later life.

In between my nights at the gym the daytime was filled with a YTS job-training course that the government stuck you on just to keep the unemployed figures down. I wasn't really enjoying it so one day I came across an advert in the local press asking for people to work at Butlin's summer camps. Within days of sending my application form away I received a call offering me the job at the Minehead camp, and to my pleasure it was the furthest one away. So I was off again!

The one thing leaving home to travel or work teaches you is independence. There's no better feeling that you can look after yourself than when you're making your own decisions and living the life you want. By this time I was still only 18 years old and I'd probably seen more of England than my parents! It was during this time that I experienced working with different accents and it was great fun, let me tell ya. Strangely enough though, as much as you love your family and friends, I wasn't missing them one bit — homesick blues – nah!

In fact I was always getting snotty letters complaining that I wasn't keeping in touch. Anyway, the summer passed with great laughs, parties, girls and a lot of hangovers. After coming back to the North I knew straight away that the bug was inside me, so living and working in my hometown was not for me. The application forms were going out thick and fast to get me on the road again.

After a couple of years moving from hotel to bar to restaurant in various towns I ended up in Bath, which was only going to be a day out for me!

At the time I was working in a hotel in Broadway, Worcestershire, and some friends of mine had arranged a job interview at a newly built country house hotel on the outskirts of Bath. Knowing that I had the same day off as them, they suggested I travel down with them, then they go to the interview before we spent the rest of the day on the piss in the city centre –great idea. So while the guys were in their interview I was across the street in the pub waiting. After a few hours I looked out of the window and caught a glimpse of the guys coming out with someone I assumed was the restaurant manager. I'd just finished my pint so I went out to meet them. As I arrived I was introduced to the manager who right out of the blue, without an interview, offered me a job along with my two mates, and being quite drunk at the time I agreed to it. So the rest of the day was spent in the city centre celebrating big time.

I was moving around a lot because I was getting bored very easily, so after I was fired from that hotel (and the next one), I started to think about moving abroad. I had a French girlfriend at the time so France sounded good but I wanted sunnier climates. It was at this time the thrill of travelling began a whole new chapter for me.

Although I was often wild and a party animal to say the least, I was good at my job, so I applied and was offered a position on board a small luxury cruise ship. I was about to experience different cultures, different languages, lifestyles, foods, climates and people everyday of my life and the funny side of it was, I was going to be paid for it – show me those palm trees!

I'd like to try and describe life at sea – unless you've been there you won't understand how difficult my task is.

To me personally, to stand on deck either day or night, but especially at night, is the most beautiful experience of freedom and independence you will ever experience in your life. To feel that warm breeze against your face and to take a deep breath of pure, fresh, clean sea air is something else. Remember when you were a kid riding your bike at great speeds downhill – did you ever take your hands off the handle bars, stretch out your arms and briefly close your eyes? (It's something I used to do being the 'crazy thrill seeking kid' as I was going down Devils Dip.) Well, that's probably the closest description I can give you. Feeling the ocean breeze rush against your face as the ship's engines take you to another country and destination is so therapeutic. We all have those memories as kids on our bikes, so the next time you're on your bike, just for a brief moment close your eyes and try to appreciate what I'm trying to describe.

(Go on... close 'em.)

As the sounds of the ocean being slashed and twisted come to the surface while we move along it is a surprisingly relaxing sound. When not attending one of the many parties in the crew area, my favourite place to be would be the back of the ship (stern), laying back in a deck chair just listening to the ocean, appreciating the peacefulness of the night and staring up at the night time sky with its stars glowing like silver Christmas tree lights. During these times nothing that this bad earth throws at you or is happening elsewhere can spoil that moment.

If you appreciate colours, then the sunsets will have you an emotional wreck; you will unashamedly gasp out loud at the brilliance that is the golden blood-red orange decorating the warm evening sky. To think that a couple of hours before the sun was a golden yellow seems unlikely as it now slowly descends into the ocean a beautiful orange colour. I swear to you the most beautiful skies you'll see are at sea. I might repeat myself a few times with that previous line throughout the chapters to come.

During my ten years at sea I discovered the world to be a big, huge place. Some places I saw made me envious of the passengers' lifestyles, some made me appreciate my own. The envy gave me encouragement to make my own world be more like theirs, but most of all to live life to the full. One day I will encourage my own children to do the same. Travel, see the world, see the sights, meet new people and even buy the tacky t-shirts and mementoes – they all come together as memories.

As fellow travellers will tell you, their most treasured possessions are their photo albums! I have a stack of photo albums at home that I wouldn't trade for the world. The whole of my young adult life is in those albums, most importantly the ten years at sea showing every sight from around the world that you can think of.

Occasionally I sit down and reflect on how my life has been filled with so much fun and enjoyment that some people don't even manage in a lifetime, and it's all down to the thrill of travelling. Besides the memories that come out of it all you've also collected addresses and telephone numbers of your good friends you made whilst travelling. Now, it's not always possible to keep in touch with them all, but it's nice, especially when you've reminded yourself of a particular person when looking through your albums, to call up and speak to him or her and ask how they are, recalling the times you had. It really does make your day when someone has remembered you and taken the time to call. 'Hey, how ya doing, I was looking at a picture of you just the other day and I was wondering how you were?' is usually the way the conversation starts.

I know even today that the bug is still inside me because as I watch today's teenagers carrying their bags or backpacks, with a copy of my book in their back pockets, I sit and stare whether it is on a train or plane, with envy. I've done my fair share but the memories still come flooding back....

The thrill of travelling.

Footnote

As I've got older and I've still got my mates up north, the thing that really bugs me is how when we get together the subject of how our lives have developed over the last twenty years or so always comes up. They all wish they could have done what I've done and really regret settling down at an early age. 'If only we'd 'ave listened to you,' is the regular reply I hear from them. One of the voices in question is my best mate Kevin. He knows what I'm about to say so he won't mind me calling him a 'plonker' again.

When we were kids growing up together, we made this promise to each other that when we were old enough to leave home we would travel and see the world.

The first leg of that tour became possible when we were both offered jobs at the summer camp I described earlier, only my starting date was a fortnight before his so I said I'd go down to check the place out. Well the rest is history for my part, but during the time away from each other Kev had met his first serious girlfriend and was head over heels in love – at 17, I ask you. Anyway, he kept to his word and followed me down two weeks later only to burn off my ears about his new love. I thought yes, this is the beginning of our worldly adventures, 'Sean & Kev's Global Chronicles'. I could see the photographers, the repaired red carpet, the B-movie budget, the cheap sparkling wine, the B&Bs and the women all gathering outside some cheap run-down movie house a few blocks down from Mann's Chinese Theatre! But after only three weeks away from his girlfriend he left me to head back north. Bloody women!

And we deliberately said 'no women'. Anyway, it used to frustrate the hell out of me for a lot of years, but as I've got older I've mellowed to the fact that it wasn't meant to be – but it would have been one hell of a road movie though. I still call him a plonker today but we have a good laugh about it and we're still the best of mates.

Two
New York

Well what can you say about New York that hasn't already been said and written or sung about? It's all fully justified let me tell ya, it's a truly fantastic place.

My first dreams of New York started when I was young and I used to admire the black and white postcards of the old *Queen Mary* sailing into old New York, with a floating army of small boats and tug boats greeting the beautiful old liner into the city. I always used to look at it and dream of doing just that – sailing into New York.

It became possible for me when I joined MS *Silvercloud*. After leaving Cork in Ireland we had seven days at sea to complete. Knowing that my dream was eventually coming true those seven days were the longest ever, and hard work I might add, as six out of the seven days where spent in mighty storms.

Our arrival time to the first sightings of land was, if I remember rightly, to be around 5.30 am. I was up bright-eyed and bushy-tailed like an excited young kid standing in line to see Father Christmas for the first time.

It was a fantastic clear morning with a bright blue sky and not a cloud in sight as we could see in the distance the Twin Towers of the World Trade Center. And the smog! A brown haze hung over the whole city like a dirty blanket; it was unreal and a shock for a few passengers who had never seen their city from afar. To our left we got our first glimpses of the lady with the torch, the Statue of Liberty and it immediately hit me – New York... wow, I've made it!

Seeing the statue makes you think of all those immigrants over the years that come to America to find their dreams and new lives. As tradition goes, for all new ships sailing into New York you get full attention from the media helicopters and the tugboats with the colourful water spray. Red, white and blue mist leaping into the morning air. It's a beautiful sight.

By now we're virtually along-side Lady Liberty and it's amazing how small she actually is. She's tiny but nonetheless beautiful, and huge for what she symbolizes. She's in my favourite ladies list, behind Lady Diana.

On the other side of her is Ellis Island where in the past all the immigrants were sent before being allowed in the country. Some stayed, some were sent home – 'Sorry guys, back to where you came from.'

Once you've sailed past her you're now approaching the impressive site of the Twin Towers and the New York skyline. On this morning, because we were greeted with a lot of sunshine, the sun reflecting off the buildings was awesome. A beautiful bright orange colour I've never seen before bouncing off the impressive structures – it was a sight to behold, one which brings a lump to my throat and still does whenever I look back at my photographs. And to think New Yorkers hated the sight of the two towers originally and even argued over the meaning of their existence. Just beyond the skyline you see the second unforgettable sight, that of the Empire State Building, which for me is what makes New York, New York, and probably the most famous of city landmarks in the world. It has stood upon its proud foundations watching the rest of the concrete jungle grow up around it and its interesting city folk walk by at its feet for years. Hell, it even withstood the jealous tantrums of a mighty chest-beating gorilla all those years ago in the black and white era.

My dreams were opening out in front of me and boy, I was chuffed so much that I couldn't resist leading a group of my shipmates to a dance as we sang, 'New York, New York'! My life-long dream had just sailed alongside me and was to remain for the next two days we were in port and boy, was I gonna go for it.

It took me quite some time to leave the city view behind me as it was breakfast time downstairs in the mess and my stomach was calling out for food. I eventually surrendered to its calling... just. The buzz going around the mess that morning was fantastic with everyone so excited being there, which like me, was the first time for a lot of other people. Being able to share that moment with other people made it all the more special. Had the mess room been full of people who had been here lots of times in the past, not finding that moment in time as special as we did, it would have been a little disappointing.

I remember walking through the crew bar area on my way back to my cabin and taking time to pause while I studied the large black and white picture frame we had hanging up. Ironically it was the same postcard print of the old *Queen Mary* sailing in to old New York.

As I stood there I remember saying to myself, 'I'm here, I finally made it.'

During my first trip ashore I experienced the New York City cab driver, which is just like the movies, believe me. And yes, you can just hold up your hand and one stops for you straight away, something I always wanted to do, just like the movies.

My driver was a Puerto Rican guy who was going crazy shouting abusive language about the state of his cab after he took over from the previous guy. He'd left junk food wrappings, plastic cups, titty magazines and cigarette butts falling out of the ashtray. He was not a happy chap, let me tell ya. He didn't really care who was in the back, he just carried on regardless throughout the whole trip, with one eye on the road, I was pleased to see. Then no sooner had I got out when he growled the price of the ride at me and then sped off with his tyres screeching! And I could still see his hand hanging out the window waving it angrily into the air.

I found the whole experience very amusing, I'm only glad the driver couldn't see me laughing while I was in the back 'cos he'd 'ave probably punched me. But I just thought to myself, 'Well, this is New York.'

My crazy driver had dropped me off at the Empire State Building where I was meeting friends of mine, Brian and Karen, who lived in the city and who I'd worked with on another ship. We had some lunch then took the incredibly fast elevator to the top of the Empire State. My God, what a view from the top of there, bloody cold and windy but beautiful. You can see everything for miles all around on a clear day, which was perfect for us.

In my early twenties, as I was then, big cities used to excite me. The buzz of the atmosphere, the noise from the car horns, the neon lights and the city people everywhere used to give me such a lift. New York was the epitome of a big, exciting city and I loved it.

Unfortunately for me my afternoon with friends was coming to an end but during my first couple of hours walking around the place I'd seen a lot and was happy to report for ship's duties.

I was to go back to New York on another occasion when I went with a Scottish couple, Robert and Caroline, who I also worked with on board *Silvercloud*. We had decided to take our vacation time together which was ten days in the 'Big Apple'.

It was also an occasion when I could meet up with Brian and Karen and introduce them to Rob and Caroline. Brian was Swedish and the best way to describe him is that he was an Elvis lookalike. Karen was English and a dancer when on board ships, but actually lived in the city looking after the family business of antiques. So while they were working I was spending all my day with Rob and Caroline, and some occasions when they wanted time together, I was able to spend the evenings with Brian and Karen. So I was getting the best of both worlds.

Anyway, one night out in a club with Brian was very memorable, to say the least. We had gone out for a few beers around the city and ended up at an old church that had been converted to a nightclub – 'The Pink Pussy' I think they called it. Maybe some of you regular visitors or locals of the city remember it? So there we were, enjoying the female scenery around us and in front of us when all of all sudden, out from the darkness, a mean-looking guy came walking towards us. I looked at this guy and thought, 'Shit, I wouldn't want to mess with him.'

But as the crowd either side of him opened out and his massive framework caught the light, it was then we both realised that he was wearing a pink ballerina's tutu and Doc Martens. Me and Brian took one look at each other and burst into uncontrollable laughter. I mean this guy would 'ave looked more appropriate in a biker's jacket with tattoos over his arms and a Harley parked outside, y'know. We had tears in our eyes as this guy came over to us and in a manly voice asked, 'What's the problem guys, you finding me funny?'

We couldn't get an answer out for blubbering and in the end the guy gave us a mean-looking stare which made it worse, 'cos how do you take a guy seriously in a pink tutu outfit? He then left to the echoes of shattering laughter. I can still hear us laughing now.

I've since been back to the 'city that never sleeps' on quite a few occasions and would have to say that it's my favourite city in the whole world. And if you use your common sense, it's not as dangerous or intimidating as it's made out to be. It's a must-see place on your travel list. I really can't explain why, but I find the place very inspiring – maybe it's the people, its history, the skyline who knows?

As ol' blue eyes used to say...

Start spreading the news.

Footnote

During the time I was writing this book the events of September 11th 2001 were taking place. I hope I have not upset anyone by recalling my memories of its fabulous skyline the way it used to be. I for one was deeply affected by seeing those once-mighty buildings being brought down like that. I never thought I'd see the day that would happen, how dare they do that to my favorite city!

God bless everyone killed on that tragic day in New York history – R.I.P.

Three
Sydney

Sydney for me was somewhere so far away I never dreamt of being able to see it. My God, it was a place on the other side of the world!

When I was a young kid at school I was always fascinated with maps, atlases and globes.

And I would love rotating a globe to countries like Australia and finding Sydney, then rotating it again and finding USA, Iceland or Norway. I loved it! But I would always wonder what it would be like to be at the bottom of the earth, as we used to say in class. Then one day it's there in front of you, right there – it's an incredible feeling. The only downfall to these ships was that you had to be up at the crack of dawn to witness these beautiful sail-ins; I guess you can't have your own way all the time, eh?

Anyway the morning was warm and a little overcast but still clear enough for good viewing. As the coastline slowly drops into the ocean you get your first sightings of the Harbour Bridge with its iron arc standing over the bay. The Opera House comes into view about now and what a beautiful sight it is. The Opera House to your left and the bridge to your right, with the city skyline towering over on both sides.

When I thought back to my school days playing with that spinning globe, the whole sight in front of me took my breath away and was taking a few minutes to sink in, 'Wow I'm at the bottom of the earth.' 'Wow' was a frequently used word by me when I was seeing all these sights for the first time. So you'll have to get used to it!

Like the New York sail-in we were greeted by a fleet of boats and yachts and an army of people standing on the water's edge. It's incredible, these people actually get up at the crack of dawn just to welcome you with a wave and a flicker of their house lights and all they ask in response is a wave back at them. 'Fair play to 'em,' I say.

And to think we would be in town for two days as well. Another 'Wow!'

The city of Sydney was a port of call during a world cruise trip while I was on board my fourth ship, the MS *Crystal Symphony*. The first half of the cruise finished in Sydney and on board for the whole of that trip was an Aussie passenger by the name of Bob Belsey from Melbourne. The guy was a really fantastic bloke, both as a passenger and a person. Day in and day out he would be sat the bar having a laugh with each member of the bar staff ('cos he thought the rest of the passengers were snobs!), and he would sit with another frequent visitor to the *Symphony* (whose name escapes me right now).

As a token of their appreciation towards the staff, he and the other guy said that when we got to Sydney they would take us all out to lunch at a fancy restaurant he knew of, all paid for. And true to their word they did! Bob faxed ahead and booked the table. I think there was about 18 of us, and what an afternoon we had – an absolutely brilliant, beautiful setting along the harbourside, in between the cruise terminal and the harbour bridge.

Two big long tables in the sunshine with both guys heading each table. They were re-ordering bottles of red and white as quickly we were drinking them. And being typical bar staff, that's exactly what we did. And we hadn't even eaten yet!

'Choose anything you want to guys and girls,' were the words coming from each head of the table. So we did! Fillet Mignon, lobster, pasta – you name it we ate it.

'More wine here for my guests,' shouted Bob. Not an empty glass in sight. We were like stuffed pigs let me tell ya.

'Desserts anyone?'

'No!' we all replied.

'More wine then?'

'Yeah okay,' came the response.

It was great fun finished off with the restaurant photographer taking table snaps. And what was touching at the end of coffee was Bob's farewell and big thank you speech, with regret that he was leaving today and a tear in his eye. But hey, we still had a couple of hours left yet, so it was off to the pubs around the trendy harbour for more drinks – and we were paying.

The funniest part of this story is that as Bob was becoming more and more pissed, the more he wanted to stay a couple more days until he reached Melbourne. So as we all staggered back to the gangway Bob had to steady himself before he could stand in front of our respectable hotel manager to negotiate a price for him to stay an extra two days. The manager agreed with a smirk on his face, as Bob was later telling us all, so everyone was happy.

As we arrived in Melbourne two days later Bob finally left and arranged for us to go to his local pub in town, The Black Prince Tavern. In there anyone who was a friend of Bob Belsey's was a friend of theirs, and was warmly welcomed. At the end we all swapped addresses with him and said our goodbyes. After two months on board with us it was like saying 'bye' to a crew member, y'know.

The poor guy was in tears again as he left the gangway. Between us bar staff we didn't look around amongst each other in fear of being spotted blubbering away ourselves!

I've got a few stories about Sydney, such as me taking a long taxi ride hoping to see a favourite boxer of mine called Jeff Fenech, only to find that he didn't train on a bloody Saturday – I was gutted! I eventually got a signed book from him though, which was nice of him.

Then on another day I had lunch alone up in the revolving restaurant high above the city on a beautiful clear day – I could see for miles it was that spectacular. But this story always stands out due to the generosity and genuine friendship that Bob got from us and we got from him.

Cheers Bob, me old mucka.

Four

St Petersburg

If you've not been to Russia before then the only way I can describe it is like stepping back in time a hundred years and into the old black and white film footage! It's a very grey and bleak place, with the streets filled with miserable, dodgy-looking people. Nobody talks to each other, looks at anyone – nothing. They just go about life in their own way. And I got the impression they don't like visitors or tourists because they know that the countries they come from are better off then they are and have more money. A very strong resentment lives within each of the locals. That's my honest opinion.

True, some of the buildings are nice, but it just seems to be the rubbish bin that the West throws away. The old trams are still in use and the old cars that are extinct in the West roam the streets of Russia, or any eastern bloc country for that matter.

Anyway, that's enough slagging the place off. It's an interesting place to visit, just to see how fortunate us westerners are. Catch it on a sunny day and you're in for a treat. Whenever we came to St Petersburg we were always sensible enough to go out in a large group, so the favourite hang-out for crew members was the Europa Hotel bar and then on to a nightclub and casino called Nevski Melodies. 'Tis very good yar.'

With the city being a very mafia-controlled place, the club was frequently used by local gangsters, but because crew members went there whenever a ship was in port they were good enough to leave us alone, knowing we were spending the Yankee dollar – which was always a relief, considering you didn't know who you were rubbing shoulders with. But that's not to say you weren't confronted sometimes by the odd drunken one – a rather nervous experience believe me, having someone shouting abuse in Russian while waving his iron fist at you! But it never lasted long as he was soon smacked and dragged away by someone carrying a machine gun over his shoulder.

Yes, that's right, I said a machine gun. It was quite a common sight considering the door staff were constantly under threat from rival gangs, also carrying guns. Afterwards the manager of the club would come over and express his deepest apologies to us, like we were VIPs. It was quite an eye-opener.

On this particular cruise, which sailed from Stockholm, we had this family on board consisting of mum, dad, teenage son and daughter. They were a real cool bunch of people but because this particular ship wasn't really catering for teenagers, the two kids were bored shitless. So the brother Danny decided to hang around the bar staff, his sister Catherine would hang out with the beauty salon girls, and because the bar was joined together with the ship's casino they would also drift between the two. Some nights we would take them downstairs to the crew bar which was warmly accepted by Ma and Pa, realising that they were looking for party people and we were the right people for the job.

With an overnight stay in St Petersburg coming up, we planned the usual trip to the Europa and Nevski's, with our two guests for company.

During the evening inside the nightclub a ship's casino girl, Lisa, who I was going out with at the time, suggested we go upstairs (I know what you are thinking) to the roulette table, where she would coach me in to winning some money. Along the way we bumped into Danny who asked if he could join us. After about an hour we were doing quite well and were on a roll, winning loads of dosh. From there we went to the black-jack table where our lady luck was to continue. 'Show me the money,' we hollered. We finished with money bulging from every pocket.

So to celebrate we ordered a couple of bottles of the best champagne to be sent over to the lounge area. Danny loved it, living it large and so were we. I don't think he'd been let loose away from Ma and Pa before so he was really going for it. And he was making new friends as well. The time was flying past and before we knew it, it was six in the morning so we decided to head for a champagne breakfast at the posh Europa Hotel.

After cheekily convincing the head waiter that we were guests of the hotel we hit the breakfast menu with a bottle of their finest champers. We pigged out big time. Anything that wasn't nailed down we ate. At the end of it, while we were finishing the last of the bubbles (hic!), for the fun of it I suggested that we do a 'runner' from the restaurant. 'Okay' was the response.

So we casually got up and because the maître d's stand was unattended, we slipped right by it and left. As if by magic there was a taxi outside the main door, so in we jumped and left. It was that simple.

All the way back to the ship we laughed. Danny had never done anything like this before, so was feeling very rebellious. 'Let's do something else,' he cheekily suggested. But the funniest thing was as we got back to the ship's gangway the passengers were leaving to go off on an excursion and who should be amongst them but Ma and Pa, who lucky for us had a big laugh out of it (although he didn't tell them what he'd just done). That rebellious attitude didn't last too long for Danny. The rest of the day for me was spent in bed as I wasn't on duty till that evening.

At the end of the cruise the parents couldn't thank us enough for looking after their son and daughter and promised that when the ship called into Rhode Island they would come to pick us up and take us to their home and serve us lunch. True enough they kept their word. In another chapter I'll explain how the day went when we arrived in Rhode Island.

'Twas very good champagne breakfast Europa, we thank you.

Five

Rio

The rich man's city and what a city it is too.

Another one of my personal dreams was to see the Christ the Redeemer statue and walk along Copacabana Beach, and here was my opportunity. Once again we were here for two days so there was no rush. Besides, I had to work most of the first day. One of the great things about working on a cruise ship is the fact that what you didn't see first time round because of work commitments, you got to see on the second visit as we always went to these ports on more than one occasion. So come the second day in town I arranged enough time off so that myself and three Swedish girls could go and check out the scenery.

One of the things I discovered before we arrived in Rio was the common mistake people make about the Christ Statue. You see, everyone I know always thought that the statue stood on top of Sugarloaf Mountain. Wrong. Sugarloaf is a completely different mountain and the actual statue stands on Corcovado Mountain. See, you learn something new every day. I'm glad I've put that common misconception to rest.

Anyway, our crew officer was good enough to give us directions and details of the helicopter that you can hire to take you all over the city tops and sights. Travelling up the steep and narrow hills in a taxi was an experience in itself. Once you reach the top the blades of the chopper are cutting slices of fresh air awaiting the pilot's green light and by now the butterflies in your stomach are racing around like crazy. Away in the distance you can see all the sights and in a few minutes we were going to be flying over them!

As the helicopter starts slowly lifting away from its pad it was an incredible feeling of being in a glass bubble. Then suddenly, without realising how high the actual mountain top we've just left was, the ground just disappears leaving us floating thousands of feet high above the city. Then as it picks up speed it nose-dives to the suburbs below. 'Jesus!' a loud voice in your head yells.

As it straightens out it's an unbelievable feeling of flying, just like a bird. The first part of the flight took us over the shanty towns, next the racecourse, then along the famous Copacabana beach filled with sun-tanned bodies, g-strings, volleyball nets and lots of potential 'Pelés'. Then the pilot took great pleasure in showing us a beautiful little cove in which there was a yacht filled with topless girls being photographed. Well, we fellas appreciated it anyway.

Waiting at the end of the beach was Sugarloaf Mountain, quite an impressive sight as it stands high and proud. But the highlight of the trip was a small figure in front of us away in the distance. Corcovado Mountain stands the highest of all the mountains surrounding Rio. To witness the beautiful sight of the Christ statue as it slowly appears in front of you is quite breath-taking. With camera at the ready, the pilot takes you around a couple of times for you to take your pictures of a lifetime. At one point he hovers above the figure's head so that you can take a shot of the view the statue is getting, as he stands high and mighty overlooking and protecting the citizens of his city. In fact the people, being very religious, will tell you that is what he is doing and the whole reason he was built.

My finger was clicking away like mad. The whole adventure was fantastic and I came away with some beautiful photographs. It's a trip everyone should take if they visit the city.

Anyway, as we circled I noticed a coffee shop at the feet of the statue so the thought of having coffee high above Rio caught my imagination. First we had to endure another one of the pilot's nose-dives back over the city towards the beach for another peek at the topless G-strings, which I didn't mind too much, as the pilot gave me a wink of approval.

Back along the coastline, then dropped off at the pad for the conclusion of our trip. It was a humbling experience getting so close to God.

The girls had to head off back to work so coffee with a view was calling out for me — 'taxi!'

At the top there you've got the usual junk shop selling its tacky souvenirs and on this occasion I couldn't resist, so I bought a stone replica of the statue. To walk the stone pathway that runs around the base of the statue is quite a peaceful walk, surprisingly, with all the tourists flocking around his feet. You get to do some serious thinking whilst leaning over the edge, taking in the view, sipping on your coffee. My usual thought was 'How lucky I was seeing all these sights and cities... and being paid for it.' Ha, Ha, Ha!

The other fun thing to experience in Rio is eating out.

We were directed to a popular restaurant called Porkau. As you are seated and expecting a menu to be placed in front of you, you are given a disk. One side of this disk is red and the other is green. Wondering where the menus are, you can now see the waiters walking around with these huge kebab-like skewers and other waiters walking with bottles of red and white wine. These guys come to your table, place the skewer down, then reach to turn over your disk to the green side and then proceed to carve off slices of meat, which on this occasion was chicken. They do this routine to everyone at the table. When he has left another guy comes over with another skewer, this time beef, slices it and places it on to your plate. This goes on and on with various choices of meat: ham, turkey, lamb, pork – you name it. Oh, and you've also got a salad bar to add to your plate for those healthy people on a diet! As the meat is taken away the guys with the wine come around and constantly fill your glass.

As the night goes on and these guys are just putting everything on your plate it becomes apparent to us that these disks are to be turned over to red whenever you are full and want time-out. When you've got your second wind you just turn it back to green and the guys with the food come back to you, simples! Great idea though. The Brits amongst us all agreed the idea would go down a treat back home in England.

When you can't eat or drink another thing they then come with the drinks trolley full of liqueurs and shooters. You come out of there stuffed as pigs and drunk as a skunk! It's ridiculously cheap as well – a fixed price per head, and I think it turned out to be $15.

Remember the place... Porkau.

Six

Mombasa

Despite the problems and poverty of Africa, the people there still welcome you with open arms and the biggest smiles beaming across their faces I've ever seen. As soon as you step off the gangway in Mombasa you are greeted by a long parade of shabby market stalls, each filled with beautiful gifts and wood carvings of lions, tigers, elephants, giraffes and tribal warriors. The artistic hard work that went into them is astonishing. And for the cheap dollars they haggle you for, it's almost embarrassing to accept. But at the same time you feel like you don't want to be ripped off by paying more then the asking price. It's crazy really, 'cos the way they are made, then polished up to a finish, you would be prepared to pay a fortune back home. These people are only asking for a fair price, yet we still haggle.

One thing I learnt about going to Africa from some of the older, experienced crew members was to always keep your old shoes. By this I mean, during a contract you can expect to go through at least two to three pairs of black shoes due to your ten to twelve hour working day, which is over and above the normal working day back home. When one pair is ruined, instead of chucking them in the bin, keep 'em. Because what might look rubbish to us is a pair of perfectly good pair of shoes to the locals of Africa and they'd be willing to pay up to $20, which is far better then wasting them in the bin, yeah. Just a little tip if you're heading for any port in Africa.

Anyway to my experience of Mombasa....

When people think of Africa for a holiday what comes to mind straight away? Yep, safari.

This was another one of my ambitions I was to achieve.

A few days prior to our arrival in Mombasa our crew officer organised a crew safari trip which included an overnight stay at a safari lodge out in the middle of the wide open bush. On a first-come-first-served basis I was in that queue like a bolt. For something that the passengers on board and people back home would be paying a fortune for, we were paying the crew officer $200. Great eh! So for all who signed up the day couldn't come soon enough.

We were picked up early in the morning by a group of Volkswagen camper vans that had the roof on hinges so it could be lifted, enabling us to stand up inside and view everything around us, and still keep the sun off our heads. Oh yeah, I forgot to tell you the heat over there is unbelievably hot, so wear something on your head and be well lotioned. After a couple of hours in hot, sweaty conditions, driving along bumpy, dusty roads we arrived at the entrance to the National Park, the first part of which you could actually walk around as it was gamekeeper controlled. Inside you can watch the monkeys, tropical birds and antelopes, amongst others. You can also walk along a pier that extends out into the river which has a glass dome under water so that you can view the hippos swimming along and, if you're lucky, a few crocodiles. But not on this day for us, though we were lucky enough to come across a baby croc – I say baby croc but it was still about five feet long with plenty of teeth and strength to rip your arm off. It was lying down in the shade beside some bushes alongside the water's edge.

I was with some Portuguese friends of mine as we all slowly took out our cameras and very carefully crept closer to get some decent pictures. Now anybody with a bit of common sense should have known that where there is a baby croc lying around, the mam and dad are sure to be close by as well y'know, protecting their young kinda thing. So what do we do, we inch ourselves even closer! Crazy gits! It's amazing how blank your common sense becomes when confronted with something so beautiful and exciting, but very dangerous (something that would happen again later on the story).

These creatures just lie there, motionless, but at any given moment could turn and snap at you with bad intentions, not forgetting that mother, on a much larger scale, could be watching from the bushes or the water's edge as well. At the time though, all we could think about was that perfect picture. There have since been times when I've sat and looked at the final picture, thought about it, and shuddered at our stupidity. Y'know you hear of these horror stories of tourists who've been attacked or eaten and I've been the first to say, 'Stupid idiots getting too close.' Hello!

After our trip around the park we boarded our vans for another trip deep into the wilderness bush, keeping our watchful eye out for the wild animals we'd come to see.

After about an hour driving slowly along the dusty roads, out from a cluster of trees without warning, comes a large male elephant followed by mother and its young. The van halted to a stop to let us admire this graceful animal. It was an incredible sight to see in its natural surroundings and an exhilarating experience that had my heart pounding like a time-bomb.

They move so gracefully for such a big animal you feel privileged to witness it all happening, but then it turned to amusement as we saw the young one was hurrying along just fast enough to keep up with its ma and pa. It was a quiet laugh mind you, we didn't want the parents to hear us! As they continued across the dirt track one-by-one they disappeared into the bush with the male parting a way through the oncoming trees and bushes. Wow... that was amazing.

We all whispered trying to contain our excitement. We couldn't wait for the next surprise, which wasn't too far down the track. This time a giraffe, another beautiful animal to see in its natural surroundings. After experiencing this first day in the bush seeing these beautiful animals, we agreed with one another that going to a zoo would never be the same, and you start to wonder whether it's right or not to actually have these animals locked up for our enjoyment.

After a day-long trek inside the camper van it was time for our driver to head off towards our lodge. It was a beautiful place with a huge open restaurant/lounge area that overlooked a popular watering hole, which as we arrived was full of a group of rather large elephants having fun bathing themselves. It was quite amusing and awesome. After taking a shower of our own and a change of clothes, we all met back at the seated lounge area.

The whole setting was beautiful and by now the sun was starting to fall slowly, creating a 'Jaffa' coloured sky. What more could I want? I was with great friends, eating well, drinking surprisingly good wine (considering our location) and about to watch a sunset under African skies (which reminded me of a Paul Simon song off the *Graceland* album which I think was called *African Skies*). I couldn't resist the opportunity of capturing the sunset on camera, as well as my table of friends.

Over the small walls of the compound the ground level dropped with a slight steepness. To the watering hole just to the right of it stood an old tree that had all its bark removed and all the thinner, smaller branches cut off until you were left with a natural-looking climbing frame.

Hanging from the highest branch wrapped in chains was a joint of meat. We were to find out that for our viewing and photographic purposes it was there to entice any leopards or lions to chew on while we watched.

As I described earlier, your common sense goes blank when faced with the excitement and danger of getting closer to a wild animal. It was after we polished another bottle of wine that we started to bet with each other about who could run down and touch the tree, then run back up and over the wall. You can imagine how crazy that must have sounded to the group of armed soldiers who were standing around the perimeter. At one time I can remember myself and two other guys actually standing on the wall ready for the guys to give us the go-ahead. How mad is that eh! If it wasn't for the girlfriends pleading with us, you never know what might have happened. We were later to find out that only one month prior to our arrival one of the waiters setting up for breakfast got dragged off into the bush by a lioness that had got through the compound wall.

After we all decided enough was enough, I can remember lying in bed and listening to the amazing sounds of the bush and its occupants living amongst it. Although they where probably a mile or so away, it seemed right outside your window. It was quite nerve-wracking, and although we were a little drunk, it still took us all sometime to get to sleep. I wasn't the only one to hear them.

But the highlight of the trip was at breakfast time. As we all sat eating our cornflakes the soldiers informed us in a quiet whisper that something was moving in the bushes below

They thought it might be a leopard. He was falling for the smell of the joint of meat that was still hanging from the tree.

'Where is he, I can't see him?' I asked.

'There, over there,' one of my friends replied.

'Wow. Look at that.'

It's surprising how big these cats really are – they are huge. It crept along very tentatively, watching everything around him. Not even the elephants having a morning wash could put him off. He was determined to get his jaws around that joint. It was as if everybody watching this beautiful animal at work was willing it to leap up the tree and start eating away. The thing was though, this was no show. We were still in the wild. We had to keep our mouths shut as he finally leapt up with two great strides to the top of the tree to his catch. You were almost tempted to give him a round of applause, but this was no circus. It was real. My only problem was I'd left my camera in my room so I've got no photos to show you... sorry.

I remember saying to myself and then to my friends, 'We're sitting here eating cornflakes with elephants to our left and a leopard eating a joint of meat straight infront of us, how cool is that eh?!'

I would have liked to have finished this chapter with a Tarzan-like roar but I wouldn't know how to spell it, so you'll just have to use your imagination!

Seven
Giza

Along with my dreams of seeing places the likes of New York, Rio and Sydney, Egypt for me represented something mystical. The aura of the pyramids and the intelligence of the old Egyptians were mind-boggling.

Some of the theories that the Egyptian people had in those days are still baffling the scientists of today, y'know. When you stand back and admire the sheer size of the pyramids and the building of these magnificent things, it makes you wonder how the hell they achieved it with no machinery, like we have today. Experts have tried replicating this feat and have failed. I'm no builder, so I'm gonna leave that to the Discovery Channel people, so anyway....

Arriving at the port of Alexandria is nothing special. It's a hot, dusty, dirty place and the locals can be somewhat annoying. But hey, this is an experience I was looking forward to so I could put up with a few things.

One piece of advice I will give is, don't let them crowd you and keep a tight hold of your bags or bum bags that you might be wearing. The locals are notorious for lifting anything and do like to try and intimidate you, especially the females of your group. So be warned.

Once you actually escape the port gates, the city itself is quite an interesting place. Just think of London with lots of dust and extremely hot conditions with the odd 'live' cow being led down Oxford Street, and it gives you a pretty good idea. But it's best for you to come and see for yourselves!

We took a bus ride which took about two-and-a-half hours, so what do we do? Crack open the beers! Along the way we visit the city of Cairo, which wasn't somewhere I was keen on seeing, but at least I could say I've been there and travelled over the Nile and visited the mosque of Muhammad Ali. Not that 'Ali', some other religious guy.

Y'know for some reason I was expecting the pyramids to stand out like Blackpool Tower, like see them from miles away. Once we'd left Cairo and entered the suburb of Giza and we still couldn't see them.

'Where are they, has somebody moved or what?' was the question on everyone's lips. Then 'Wow!' All of a sudden there they are, right in front of you, standing tall and... old. What an awesome sight they are. It's almost overwhelming. To think that they've been built for thousands of years is incredible, even standing longer than the Rolling Stones. And to think, as I said earlier, they've baffled even the most intelligent scientist – the pyramids not the Stones. Mind you, I wouldn't be surprised to hear Keith Richards was a labourer on the site!

After leaving the sanctuary of the lovely cool air-conditioned tour bus, the desert heat just hits you in the face, it's stifling. And it's quite a walk to the first interesting sight which is the ruins of the Sphinx with its broken nose. Rumour has it, or so the tour guide will have you believe anyway, that Napoleon was responsible for breaking off the end of its nose. Well you never know, it could be true? Nevertheless, an impressive piece of workmanship. And it felt like it was getting hotter!

I guess it's a sign of the times, but one thing that made me laugh when looking at the pyramids from a distance, before making the journey to them, was the fact that they've got a main road that runs right between them, cats' eyes an' all. Now I'm no historian, but I'm almost sure the old Egyptians weren't responsible for the roads as well!

But when in the desert do as the locals do – see the sights on a camel. Before that day I'd never even been close to a camel, so meeting one face-to-face was an experience. They have got to be one of the smelliest animals on this earth, they stink! And they've got extremely bad breath to go with it, but hey, I didn't complain with the dirty taxi cab in New York, so I wasn't going to grumble now.

The biggest fun is getting on the bloody thing and making sure you're properly comfortable before the guide yells at the camel 'Up!' If not you can kiss your arse goodbye 'cos you'll be sent flying over the handlebars, so to speak. Which is amusing from afar, but not for the person involved, so another piece of advice is get yourself comfy fairly quickly because the guide won't wait for you, they love to embarrass you!

Oh I forgot to say, before you mount up they dress you up in the typical robe and turban and take your picture of you looking like an extra from *Lawrence of Arabia*. Once you get going it's quite a ride, especially if you're like me and have had horse riding experience, it's no different really. But it's funny watching others.

Once that's out the way and you've climbed down, you've got the Great Pyramid looking over you and you start to appreciate the actual size of it. Then start thinking back to those numpty scientists again.

I think the one thing that struck me was the actual size of each block – each solid stone block – and how huge they were. And without the use of today's mechanics, how the hell did they lift them into place? To actually see them is absolutely incredible!

You can't praise and admire the Egyptians enough. You have to physically climb each stone block and God knows the amount of passageways and tunnels that are inside. One of the highlights of the tour is that you can actually go deep down inside and walk around an old catacomb with some old writings on the walls (I'm not even going to embarrass myself by try to spell the word they use for Egyptian writing). But you can't stay in there long because the heat inside is hotter then the outside and there's not much air down there either, believe me. So the climb back up the steep broken steps towards the pinhole exit that gets bigger as you climb towards it is quite a welcome sight. 'Water, water!' is the only thing on your mind!

After you've taken your usual group shots with the pyramids in the background, and drunk lots of water, it's the markets stalls that you find yourself being taken to by the guide, who is probably working on a percentage with the owners of them. Here you'll find beautiful stone carvings of Egyptian gods, one of which stands in my hallway, and the usual necklaces and bracelets.

To carry on the historical theme of the day we headed off to the Egyptian Museum. Inside is a collection of beautiful artefacts that have been found over the many years that people have been digging in and around the pyramids. Some of them range from some small jewellery to large (and I mean large) stone carvings of the Egyptian sons, through to old chariots and gold thrones. All of which have all been beautifully preserved. Saving the best 'till last they take you into a room full of all the gold that was found, the highlight being he mask of Tutankhamen. Solid gold and pure breath-taking beauty! I must say it felt a privilege to be there and to see something that old, yet still so beautiful and priceless was quite a feeling. And it's only visible to you by way of armed guards everywhere.

After the tour we wandered on down through the streets to the Gold Market, which was ready and waiting to welcome our American dollars with big cheesy smiles on their faces.

In there you can get anything in gold that you want. As part of the deal of getting us in there we were offered gold pendants to hang from our gold chains with our names written in gold Egyptian writing. It was a hagglers paradise! All part of the experience of visiting the pyramids I guess.

Anyway, after we bought everything that wasn't nailed down we headed off back to our bus to start our long trip back to the ship. Waiting for us on board was a bunch of ice coolers filled to the top with beers! We were prepared. Well you have to be with weather conditions sapping the fluids out of you. The trip back was loud and drunken but an extremely good way of finishing off a perfect day, one that I'll never forget.

Cheers Giza!

Eight

Cannes

From one extreme to another. Giza, a hot, dusty dirty place with the pyramids as a backdrop, to Cannes, a hot, stylish, rich resort of the South of France. That's how different your scenery can be within a matter of days while on board ship. It's great, and we get paid for it as well, don't forget.

Everything that you can imagine about a place where the rich and famous like to hangout is right here in Cannes. The flashy cars, the large yachts, the exclusive hotels and the leggy women. The place stinks of money. Seeing how they live and play really makes you feel envious. But my friends and I were going to have a bit of expensive fun our way.

During a crew party the night before we arrived in Cannes I was talking with some dancer girlfriends. I discovered that they'd arranged a day out on board some yachts they'd hired. As the night progressed one of the male dancers cancelled his place. Without hesitation one of my girlfriends came to me and asked if I wanted to buy his place. 'Well aye, of course,' was my quick reply.

I quickly re-arranged my working shift with one of the other bartenders, costing me $100, so then I was set. Money talks on board these bloody ships y'know. It was going to be worth it though.

Even though we had to be up around 7.30 am it didn't stop us partying the night away like true party animals. After meeting for breakfast in the mess to get rid of the hangovers, we set off to the harbour to meet our playboy toys.

They had hired two yachts capable of carrying ten people and wine and lunch was included. The trip would take us up and down the Riviera coastline stopping off at various idyllic spots for swimming. And what a spectacular day for it was too. It's amazing the effect that sea air has on the old hangovers.

And to think some of these playboys get to do this everyday if they want to, we were making the most of it for just one. So the suntan lotion came out, the shades were put on and the G-strings were twiddled with. We were determined to live it large, if only for a day. Our yachts came with cooks and captains, so all we had to do was relax and get 'smutty'. Let's just say a lot of flesh was exposed that afternoon. But I won't go into that, that's another book.

Lunchtime arrived before you knew it, which was nice. Pasta, salad, cheeses, fish, ham, French bread and lots of Chardonnay. Then the typical water fights followed. The whole day was one big laugh after another; it was superb I was very grateful for the girls inviting me along – merci!

After the events of the previous visit to Cannes our next trip included an overnight stay, which are always great fun and have been know to get very messy.

When it comes to time off on board ship, especially the overnighters, it's very simple. Management don't care what you do when your shift has finished, as long as you are not involving the local police or drugs, and that you are on duty on time the next day, clean-shaven, clean uniform and sober. It's that simple!

It's a common thing to be sent complimentary tickets from the local nightclubs whenever a ship is in port. On this occasion our crew officer received tickets from a club who had organised a huge party on the beach grounds of the famous Carlton Hotel. Wicked eh? I say 'beach grounds' because every hotel along the front there has its own section of beach, strictly for its hotel guests.

There were barbeques, cocktail bars, guest DJs playing thumping dance music (which is not normally my taste but for one night I was dance crazy) and performers walking around on stilts. Everybody was having a great time and you either danced where you stood or you climbed on to these seven feet tall platforms and danced high above everyone - it was unreal and definitely the place to be in Cannes that night. It was a beautiful warm evening, plenty of beer and vodka and French girls. (I'll let you in on a secret: I've got a weakness for French girls so I was in 'ohhlala' heaven.) Still, didn't see anyone famous though. Saying that, I could have been dancing next to Brad Pitt and I wouldn't have noticed.

To finish off the night, at around four in the morning they had a big colourful firework display, which lit up the star-filled sky beautifully.

As you can imagine there were a few 'hanging' people amongst the crew the next day but as I said, management don't care as long as you are doing your job to a five star standard — yeah right!

I would have to say that Cannes is one of my favourite places — it's wild, colourful and anything goes! I've been there on quite a few occasions and I've always had a blast.

Magnifique.

Nine

Port Douglas

When thinking of Australia people like myself think sharks, Neighbours, Fosters and the Great Barrier Reef. Port Douglas offered us the chance to enjoy at least one of the mentioned, the Barrier Reef. Anybody who learns to dive has one ambition and that would be to dive in the most famous reef in the oceanic world. We were novices and beginners to scuba diving and we were about to have the opportunity millions would die for.

This was happening during some extended time off whilst on board my first ship, the MS *Song of Flower*. At the time we were about to sail from Singapore on a seven day cruise to Cairns, Northern Australia. Our passenger capacity for a full ship would be 220, but for our first trip to Cairns we only had 105 passengers and for the return leg back to Singapore we only had 112.

So the captain and the hotel manager sat down and discussed the situation and came to a generous conclusion that they would grant the first half of crew members seven days off for the first half of the trip and the second half of the crew seven days off for the return leg of the trip. This won great appreciation from all crew members, considering that when we signed our contract for the job it stated that you work an average of ten hours a day, seven days a week for six months with no days off. So to be given seven days off was unheard of!

Here we come Oz!

Port Douglas itself is a typical little tourist place and the only thing going for it is the fact that the reef is only a few miles out to sea. It looks very man-made, what with your tacky t-shirts and souvenir shops everywhere. Not many genuine Aussies around really.

We paid our fees and were taken on board our Quicksilver catamaran. If I remember rightly, the trip out to the location took us almost an hour, so we had plenty of time to relax, enjoy the trip and take a crash course for all of 30 minutes on scuba diving. Our instructor went through all the hand signals, the equipment and how to empty our mask should it become filled with water, as well as how to move in the water without disturbing the reef – after all it is a living thing. All of this in 30 minutes! 'What was the signal for shark again?!'

We finally arrived at our platform out in the middle of nowhere, equipped with a viewing gallery and coffee shop, to start our adventure with the deep. The excited butterflies were out in force causing a storm within my stomach. After a quick reminder of the hand signals etc., we were kitted out with our flippers, masks, belt and tanks (which almost flip you over onto your back with the weight of them). We certainly looked the part anyway. We took up our seats upon a bench that was lowered into the water. Alongside me were my friends Eugene (a Dutch guy), Francesco (a Portuguese guy) and sweet Mary (an English girl), oh and a cameraman who comes along with you to film your experience. While we were having our 'crash course' chat our instructor told us to breathe normally rather than panicking and holding our breaths when entering the water. 'Your body will immediately remember back to when it was in your mother's womb,' he said.

All this is flashing through your mind as the water is getting closer. 'Okay breathe... just breathe,' you repeat to yourself. Within a few seconds it's true, your body does adjust. It's amazing, a real thrill to think you don't have to rush back to the surface for another deep gulp of air. After we all gave the thumbs up to each other, away we went swimming with the 'fishies'. Beautiful shapes and all colours, all swarming around you – and some of them give you a little nip just to check you out, to see if you're edible I guess.

It's a fantastic feeling as you start kicking with your flippers to move gracefully along with them. And with little effort these little guys either side of you dart from left to right with flashes of speed. And they're all curious what's inside the mask as they try to rub noses with you. I wouldn't recommend it, you feel uneasy with them being so close, but I found it a beautiful and hilarious feeling, almost tickling. And the feeding frenzy that goes on as soon as the instructor brings out some scraps of food for them is chaos.

The unspoilt beauty of the reef with all its colours surrounded by the crystal clear turquoise water is out of this world, really breath-taking. And it's all living as well — it's amazing!

And it was all being caught on camera for us too.

During the tour of the sea bed, which was 30 meters below us, we came across one of those huge clamps – or do they call them clams – I can't remember. Our guide waved us over to take a look. One by one we came over to notice that its huge jaws were open. The position I took up was directly above this thing when all of a sudden I began to slowly sink towards it. I could see this huge living thing licking his lips at me. For fear of smashing the coral beneath me I didn't want to start frantically kicking with my flippers, so the guide reached out and grabbed my scruff and pulled me back up. It was all caught on camera as well – it was a good laughing point when we reached the surface later.

We were down there exploring the bed for about 40 minutes which wasn't long enough. I can see why people get hooked on this scuba diving. It's so peaceful and unspoilt by man and the colours are so sharp. I could have stayed down there for hours.

Before leaving, our cameraman prompted us to perform in front of the camera so we took it in turns to throw ourselves into slow motion somersaults. It was greeted with a big thumbs up from everyone. Needless to say the rise to the surface was a sad one. The rest of the day was spent doing the next best thing, snorkelling. But it doesn't have the same effect anymore once you've done the 'scuba'.

At the end of the day we were given copies of the tape of our experience which we later added the soundtrack from *The Big Blue* movie to. We were also given a certificate stating that we'd dived the Agincourt Reef, which lies proudly in one of my photo albums. It's a lovely videotape of a day I'll never forget and has become one of my prized possessions. And to think that many experienced divers never get the chance to dive the reef at all, here I was a complete and utter beginner doing it on my very first one!

A big thumbs up.

Ten

Alaska

When I first started filling in application forms for my first ship, I would often find myself sat in a coffee shop window people watching and just day-dreaming about these places far away and exotic. So you can imagine the excitement I felt when I was ripping open the envelope containing my first contract.

'Yes,' I was thinking, 'I'm off... sunshine, beaches, women and cocktails.' I was gutted when I realised that the contract was for a summer in bloody freezing Alaska! 'What's going on 'ere, is this a joke or what? I'm supposed to be going somewhere sunny and nice, not Alaska!'

My mates couldn't stop laughing – they gave me so much stick for it. So there we were, me and my French girlfriend Valerie, standing at the ticket desk of Heathrow, bags packed and ready to fly out to Vancouver, Canada.

Anybody reading this that has experienced Alaska on board a ship will tell you of the capital Janeau and its famous Red Dog Saloon, or the Lucky Lady bar just down the street, or the Ketchikan café famous for its steak and pancakes breakfast. Many a drunken night was to be spent in these places during the summer – great fun!

But away from the social side of Alaska is the scenery. It is absolutely 'awesome', as our American friends would say. This is why I'm dedicating this chapter to the country itself, instead of one particular place or events.

The snow-topped mountains dwarf the rivers, lakes and towns. They make these huge cruise ships look like little tug boats, and it really wasn't that cold either. It's a strange feeling though, to be out on the crew sundeck sunbathing with your headphones on, to see a small iceberg or ice pack with a family of seals sat on top come floating past you. It was all very surreal as you rubbed more lotion on to your arms, sipping a cold beer.

Although the week's cruise became very familiar to crew members, some of the beauty spots the ship would go to never became boring. Every week we would go to a place called Adolphis Point, which was a gathering place for the blue whales. These beautiful mammals used to love the attention they got so would come in their dozens. To see these graceful creatures in their natural habitat made you feel really lucky to see them, but then the thought of them being hunted and killed by man would make you feel sick. It's a real shame.

The best moments to see are when this huge frame is leaping out of the water and then comes crashing down with enormous eruptions of water. It's called breeching. It really is amazing, it's like it's happening in slow motion. The passengers and crew loved it. I never managed to catch any on camera though, which was a shame. They never were very good at letting us know when they were about to breech.

On another day we would sail into a huge bay at the foot of a glacier – not too close mind – and watch the ice packs lose their grip and collapse away from the glacier edge with an almighty bang as they hit the water below. It's an awesome sight to see and this time I did manage to get some shots on camera. On some days though, if the ice packs weren't falling right on cue, the captain would sometimes blow on the ship's horn and cause movement himself. He wasn't actually supposed to do it but I'm sure these rich Americans used to pay him a few hundred dollars to make it happen.

Towards the end of the summer myself and a group of friends hired a helicopter to take us over the Alaskan landscape and the glaciers. Without sounding like I'm repeating myself the words 'awesome', 'spectacular' and 'fantastic' immediately come to mind – unbelievable sights!

The views are outstanding and are more approachable in a helicopter I think. The way the pilot took us in and out of some of the cliff edges was a big thrill, y'know. Flying over tree tops at great speeds, then coming down almost to ground level chasing the moose along the green fields and across the rivers, was great fun. Then back up amongst the mountain tops within seconds is just like a roller coaster ride. There was certainly a lot of screaming from the girls behind me. To finish off the trip the pilot landed on top of a glacier, which was quite a unique experience. To think these things actually shape valleys and have been frozen for thousands of years. I wonder how many people can say that they've actually walked on a glacier eh? I have!

At the end of my contract I remember sitting in a bar in Vancouver, Richards on Richards (on Richards Street) or 'Dick on Dicks' as it was known to the locals, and recalling what I thought when I first got my contracts through saying Alaska for six months. At the end of it I was thinking, 'I've come away with some great memories and experiences from here.' I'm glad I chose to put in my Alaska chapter because the whole place is spectacular and I take back everything I said about the place beforehand. My mates certainly weren't laughing anymore when I showed them my photographs, my suntan and told them my stories.

Everybody I've met during my travelling years, both passengers and crew, all talk about Alaska with great fondness. I'd happily go back tomorrow if I could.

It's a beautiful place to see.

Let's just hope it stays that way.

Eleven
Hong Kong

Well, well, well so I've finally got round to Hong Kong. I had an experience there that I'll never forget! But I won't start this chapter with that story just yet though, because I want to highlight the beauty of the city first.

We would sail into Hong Kong on quite a few occasions, and to this day the city skyline impresses the hell out of me every time I see it. The place is an architect's dream.

You could quite easily pass it for a city in some sci-fi movie of the 21st century, using it as a backdrop. It is stunning — well I think so anyway. The magnificent splendour of these sky-reaching buildings is a sight to see. And they look so close together as well, you find it impossible to think that six lanes of main roads pass between them. God forbid Godzilla should choose the place to have a battle with some other prehistoric dude and topple over a few skyscrapers, starting a domino effect all round the harbour.

At the foot of every building is a remarkable blend of old and new. The streets are draped with flags and advertising bunting stretched from building to building which gives it a real far-eastern flavour. And in between some of these huge towers stands some smaller one-storey buildings selling old Chinese antiques, suits or medicine herbs from old Chinese wise men. Then on the next corner you'll find all the designer shops and boutiques with the mega dollars associated with them. Oh, and watch out for the crazy traffic too. It's no different over there than it is here, or a big city in the States.

But it's great fun and a really lively place to be in. Big cities always give me a huge buzz and this rates with the best of them. And you have to take a Star ferry across the harbour to get that all-round view – that's if you didn't sail in on a five star ship already.

The highlight after the days spent in Hong Kong has to be the champagne midnight sail-aways. To see the skies lit up with stars against a royal blue background, with a forefront of towering skyscrapers, also lit up, is absolutely breathtaking. And so colourful with all the neon lights everywhere and the office lights within each building beaming so brilliantly. The electricity bill must be as high as the tallest building. No wonder Chris Patten was kicked out because he kept running up a huge bill!

But anyway, on to my story, and I'll start by telling you this is the truth, the whole truth and nothing but the truth, so help me God!

I had just about had enough of England and its shitty weather so I applied for another contract at sea. I had sent off forms to various companies, then sat in wait. One day the postman brought me a letter which offered me a job on board the MS *Southern Cross*. I was that desperate to leave I accepted and was due to fly out of Heathrow, bound for Hong Kong. For some reason during the whole time from accepting the job onwards this little voice in my head was telling me 'don't go', but against my better judgement there I was window seat, non-smoking, supping free wine and looking forward to some sunny pleasures courtesy of Bali and Australia. Wrong!

I can't remember exactly how we met, but on board my plane and two rows in front of me was another English guy, who was also going out to this ship. So one thing led to another and we got chatting. The next thing you know we're polishing off large quantities of wine together. Great. We introduced ourselves somewhere in the conversation – his name was Simon Hale, from Liss in Hampshire, a great guy.

Although the cruise industry is a huge business, it's a very small world within it. We both didn't know much about this ship we were going to, apart from what we had seen in the glossy brochures we had been sent. Sound suspicious yet?

The other experience of Hong Kong is flying into its airport. Wow! It is unbelievable. As you start to descend from out of the clouds, the city and its suburbs just appear below you with such frightening quickness you hardly have time to enjoy the aerial views. During the last miles to the runway you literally fly over tower blocks which are people's homes, almost clipping off the tops of them. Then as the city approaches you can see down in between the buildings and towers to the people on the streets below. How on earth the pilot controls things is beyond me. One slight mistake and a big portion of the downtown area will disappear. I think from a pilot's point of view it must be the most daunting yet thrilling, dangerous airport to fly in and out of.

After surviving the landing we were both met at the airport by the ship's agent who loaded us into his car to take us to the harbour. Fine, no problem. Upon arriving at the dockside we were dropped off in front of this big and ugly red ship that was old and really dirty. At the bottom of the gangway we were greeted by the ship's crew officer, 'Hello, welcome', the usual shit.

It was plain to see that it was an old ship from the old era with its polished wooden interiors and 'naff' décor. It was all very grand, better on the inside than the outside, but not really my cup of Darjeeling.

We were taken to the hotman's office (a ship's term for the hotel manager) to sign our contracts, etc. First big mistake!

From there down to the crew area to get acquainted with the rest of the ship and its crew. Second big mistake!

As we entered the crew area the stench of shit and more shit just hit us both, it was disgusting. And it was over 100 degrees down there. As we walked through the corridors we couldn't help but notice the debris of rotten fruit and veg covered in flies all over the place. As it was being cooked in the heat it was probably a good source of the smells.

'Surely it gets better than this?' I said to Simon.

'Let's see what the crew mess is like,' he replied. Third big mistake!

Remember in the old movies where our hero would walk into a bar he knew he wouldn't be welcome in because the place was crawling with gangsters and killers? Well, that is the nearest description I can give for this crew mess. It was dark, dirty, and hot, and filled with dodgy-looking geezers who followed you everywhere with their eyes.

Looking at our surroundings and its members we could have done with a stiff drink but we settled for coffee instead. Well, it looked like coffee. We didn't dare ask for something to eat!

While we were sat there discussing our next move we could feel their eyes burning in to the back of our heads. It was then that we decided that we weren't staying. So now what?

'I know, let's go and check out the crew cabins just out of curiosity.'

Walking down the corridor towards the cabin area we both noticed the communal showers, which just goes to show how old the ship was. These days your cabin has its own shower and we'd never heard of communal showers before. I guess you could say we'd both been spoilt by our previous ships. Walking on we came to the cabins and by pure luck we came across the two bartenders we were replacing as they were packing bags. One guy was Portuguese, the other Polish. The Polish guy was at the end of his contract but the Portuguese was leaving early because he couldn't stand it anymore.

'Why?' I asked. He started to explain about the conditions on board, and how most of the crew members, mostly the officers and engine department, were fighting and stabbing each other all the time. Unbeknown to us before we came out, 90% of the crew were from the divided Soviet Union, Yugoslavia and Croatia! My God, no wonder there was warfare on board. If they can't live together on land what makes you think they'll be happy with each other at sea? Oh, and in between there were a few Greeks and Turks! No need to explain that one.

Days before arriving in Hong Kong the engine department went on strike, leaving the ship stranded at sea for a day before the problem was solved, something to do with unpaid wages. The crew bar was open just one night a week because of the constant fisticuffs. And the last time it was open there was a stabbing!

The actual cabin stunk of blocked drains, the fittings were falling apart and the Polish guy took great pride in showing us his pet cockroach called 'Peter'. I'm not kidding you, it's as true as I'm sat here writing it.

'Okay we've seen enough, let's go.'

On our way up to the hotman's office we had to decide for sure that we were going to stand by each other on this because we knew the management wouldn't be too pleased with what we had to say.

We were pretty damn sure we were not leaving on that dirty floating shit-hole.

Going back to our first mistake, when we signed our contracts, we also handed over our passports. Doh! So we both knew somewhere along the conversation the word 'immigration' would be dropped in. Sure enough the hotman was not amused and tried really hard on persuading us to stay, at least to Sydney, which was only five days away. We stood by our decision and firmly replied 'No.' From that point on the air turned nasty and a lot of threatening words were used, even the suggestion of having us arrested and handed over to immigration police for jumping ship. We were asked to leave the office and re-think this. We were prepared for this because effectively 'jumping ship' is what we were doing. Which is why we made a strong agreement to stand by each other just to get us off the ship – then we'd worry about the next problem when we came to it. We were summoned back after about 10 or 15 minutes to hear our fate.

Considering the fact he could have handed us over to the police we were given a pretty good deal. He agreed to hand over our passports – fine — but he had, by law, to inform immigration of our identities and the reasons for us leaving our contracts. Shit!

The thing was though, he'd already done this while we were outside his office and the immigration police were on their way over to the ship. So it was a crazy situation to be in – there we were scrambling around to find our bags whilst the law was on their way over to arrest us. Anyway we managed to get the hell off the 'shit-hole' of a ship and clear the terminal before they got there. Phew!

Throughout the years Simon and I had been travelling we had become familiar with Seamen's Missions. These are places where sailors from either merchant, cargo or naval ships could go to stay cheaply for the night or hang out at the bar, get something decent to eat, send post home or make a phone-call. You name it, you could find it at these places. And they are usually run by people of the church. So we decided to look for such a place. And luckily enough we found one only a short walk from the terminal.

This particular place was run by a priest called Father Peter, bless him. We sat down with Father Peter and told him the whole story of the sticky predicament that we had found ourselves in. He was very understanding of our story and so agreed to help us. First he arranged for us to stay at the mission for free for as long as it took to get us home, then organised something for us to eat whilst he made a few phone calls to immigration.

He came back later to let us know that things were being seen to. During our chat with the Father, I noticed bit of a familiar accent so I asked him where he was from. To my surprise he said he was born in Hartlepool but spent a lot of his time working at a church called St Mary's in Stockton-on-Tees, my home town! I couldn't believe it, but what made it all the more extraordinary was the fact that my mother worked there helping the elderly people. Father Peter knew her and remembered her. Can you believe it eh, you come to the other side of the world and meet a guy from your hometown that has worked with your mum?! (It doesn't stop there though.)

The rest of the day passed without incident so we thought it best to phone home and tell our families of the situation. Imagine the surprise my mother got when I told her of Father Peter. In reply she asked me to ask Father Peter of his mother's name, and to let her know whenever I got to a telephone the following day. Simon called his family and told them of our chance meeting, and assured them everything was okay.

The following morning Simon had gone downstairs to ask his girlfriend if she could wire him some money for us to live on for a couple of days. I had just got up and was lazing around when all of a sudden I could hear this loud screaming and something being kicked. I quickly got dressed to arrive on the scene with Father Peter and saw this immigration officer kicking at the glass door with Simon sat inside as he was talking to his girlfriend, trying to arrest him!

There was trouble everywhere. Poor Simon had got hold of the door on his side tightly while his girlfriend was shouting down the phone, as the officer was trying to kick the glass in and drag Simon away — the guy was in tears. Anyway, the officer was ordered out of the building as Father Peter was explaining to him that the situation was being taken care of. He eventually left but was still determined to have us both. Simon finally came out of the booth but was shaking like a leaf. After a few seconds we both gave out this loud, but very nervous and relieved laughter. A few minutes later the Father came back into the building to tell us that things were okay but to watch ourselves if we went outside. Yeah right!

After everything had calmed down I asked Father Peter what his mother's name was and told him that my mother had sent her regards. I think it was something like Ethel and when I spoke to my mum again I told her. She informed me that my Auntie Eunice is now looking after her while she is in hospital, unbelievable eh?! Not only do I meet this guy from my hometown up north, I find out that he's also worked with my mother, and that my auntie is now looking after his sick mother in hospital, while we are in bloody Hong Kong where he now lives. And it's all a true story of incredible fate!

During all of these discoveries Simon just sat there in amazement. 'Unbelievable,' he says.

So for the rest of the day we both kept our heads very low, never walking as far as the front steps. Father Peter later informed us that his friend at immigration had got us cleared of any wrong doings and we were okay with the law. Phew!

The next thing he has to work on is our transport home, because as we were both coming to a new job we didn't have a lot of money in our pockets. Fortunately Simon's girlfriend sent him some money for the next couple of days we were going to be in town. We thought what the hell, we might as well start enjoying ourselves, as you do. So we spent a few nights getting rather drunk and telling our story to people we met while we were out and about. They seemed to get a laugh out of it, as I hope you are while reading it.

I think it was the fifth day when Father Peter came to us and told us he'd arranged our flights home for the following day, for which we were very grateful. I'll never forget what he did for us both or the experience of Hong Kong. He took us to the airport and said our goodbyes with a big hug. I've since been back there quite a few times and hold no bad memories of the place – in fact I recommend people go there – it's a great place.

As for Simon and me, well we took advantage of the complimentary wine on the way back to Heathrow and promised to keep in touch after separating at the airport with a mighty hug for each other, and said it was a pleasure being on the run with each other. We eventually lost touch but funnily enough I was on a new ship in Venice enjoying some time off, having a beer with my new shipmates, and tied up alongside our ship was a Princess ship.

There I was enjoying myself when this figure walks off the gangway of the Princess ship and starts walking towards this same bar that I'm sat in. To my surprise I recognise the figure to be Simon. I stand up and give a big hello to my 'ship-jumping' buddy. 'How the devil are ya?' we asked each other. I introduce him to my mates and we end up telling the story to them as we polish off quite a few beers and vodka that afternoon. We eventually both staggered off to our ships to report for duty completely pissed. I don't know about Simon's, but my manager wasn't too pleased with me when I got back! Cheers Simon!

A big 'Thank You' to Father Peter.

Twelve
Saigon

During my years at sea I've been to some amazing places. Some of them poverty had struck, some of them were 'stinking' of money. But not in my wildest dreams did I ever think I would be going to a place like Saigon, Vietnam. So much history attached to the place, the centre of all the bloody stories and grief stricken people, both Vietnamese and Americans. The centre of all the political troubles and the scene of one of history's biggest evacuation plans. The centre of where it all began all those years ago. Wow, this is Saigon!

So many young people from both sides unnecessarily killed, and especially the young men from the States fighting people they had no quarrel with. It was all wrong and should never have happened. But hey, I'm a traveller, not a politician.

As for the country itself, it's beautiful and green, and the people are amongst the friendliest you'll ever wish to meet. I guess some of the buildings have been left in the same condition as the war left them with bullet holes, and some of the roads left with craters in the middle. Either that, or the country is so poor it's not had the cash to repair them. But all around you can see evidence of battle scars both structural and physical. Some of the people still carry the burden of handicap that was given to them against their request. And some of the sad children remind you of what it might have looked liked seeing the children of then walking the streets, looking for their dead mothers and fathers only to find poverty and refuge amongst the rubbish that people had thrown away, or the ruins of their family homes. It's all a very sad place, but it has a certain beauty about it – I can't explain what exactly.

The day we arrived I managed to pay someone to work for me so that I could see the place for myself along with my Italian friend Andrea. Outside the port gates you will always find yourself a lift, whether it be a push bike, car, tuk-tuk, carriage or an old motorbike. On this occasion they were standing there with their mopeds. So

Andrea and I started haggling straight away with two guys willing to take us around town for the day for the bargain price of 10 or 15 dollars – I can't remember exactly. But they are there with you everywhere, all day, and even carry your shopping on the back of the bike. And they make sure you're not getting ripped off as well, and best of all they keep you away from the rest of the tourists. This is great because some of the best places to go to are off the tourist trail, taking you to the real people and places of the city y'know. It's not always possible in some cities though. It's just being careful of those places in the cities or countries you can go too. You learn as you go along I guess, and listening to other travellers or crew members is always recommended. But in Saigon I never felt threatened once. I wish I could say the same about other places though.

So there we were, flying through the streets on the back of these noisy mopeds, churning out black smoke behind us, being greeted with a smile and a wave from the locals. Finally arriving at the best restaurant that Saigon had to offer, or so our drivers told us. Not much to it really, it was open to the streets from both sides and had flower tiled flooring.

On one of the walls were pictures of old sixties movie stars and on the other it had picture frames of Wham! But the food was great and the bottled cokes were chilled, and that's all you can ask for really in that heat. The heat is stifling and you are always reminded to consume as much fluid as possible. The locals look at you like you're 'softies' y'know, having a laugh or two at our expense as we stagger around sweating buckets. 'Slanty-eyed gits!' we would call them as we chuckled amongst ourselves.

After the refreshments it's back to the road to find a great market place, a haggler's heaven. The art of haggling is learnt as you go along travelling from country to country. Never ever accept the first price (rule number one). Always half his first price (mentally) then half it again as your first offer. He will give you the customary, 'Ha, ha, ha, you must be joking my friend. Higher, higher give me better price.' You reply by walking away shaking your head, 'Nah sorry mate, too high for me I'm afraid.'

You can guarantee he'll let you walk away so far then call you back. Rule number two, never go back straight away, always pause for a few minutes before you reluctantly start slowly walking, as if at a crossroads.

'Okay, okay. You give me better price. I want to do business with you, come on.'

That's when he's ready for the taking. So you offer him the first price again, or if you are real callous you can offer half of the half price just to see his reaction. He'll probably laugh at you again or even curse you, but then he'll start just above the asking price you offered the first time, waiting for you to either accept or to try and come down in price once more. If you really want to take the piss then walk away muttering to yourself, 'Nah sorry, I can get it for my asking price down the street off another guy.'

That's the bit that really upsets them, they go crazy! Shouting abuse and waving their hands all over the place. Rule number three – never let them intimidate you by all his hand waving and abuse. Stand brave and smile. It can be good fun in some places I've been to, especially in Istanbul. They will spend hours if necessary to get you to take their offer, and they'll even have tea made for you. But some places in Turkey I've been physically escorted out of the shop and had the door slammed behind me. Ha, ha, ha! It was all good fun. So anyway back to our haggling....

After he's calmed down he will nine times out of ten accept your offer and always give you his life story of how you are depriving his family by buying his goods at a ridiculously cheap price (yawn!). Don't let your conscience get the better of you though, because he can always get his money back from the passengers off the ship, especially the Americans. And you walk away knowing that you've got yourself a bargain without being ripped off. And that my good friends, is the art of 'haggling'.

I can't remember everything I bought that day, but I do remember buying a mandolin for my friend Mike, who is a guitar player in Bath. It sounded really good when I got home to give it to him. I wonder if he still has it - he'd bloody better have, it took me ages to haggle a good price for it!

The day was really passing quickly and the sun was starting to fall, releasing magical orange colours over the ruined city – it looked beautiful.

My only regret of the day was not going to the War Remnants Museum. So many people went and came back with good stories of the place and how interesting it was. I felt a little gutted about it really. But I made a decision not to go because I didn't want to see the horrors of war with all its death and destruction. We all know it was a disaster, with no one coming out of it with any credit or respect. So why would I want to see the place where America and its politicians made its biggest cock-up!!

The saddest and most upsetting part of the day for me was when our drivers dropped us off at the port gates. The two guys couldn't do enough for us. They carried our bags right to the gang way, you could see they were trying hard for a tip. So it came to paying up time. I reached into my pocket and brought out the agreed money and placed it into the hands of my driver (whose name I've forgotten).

'Thank you Mister Sean, thank you,' was his reply.

In my other pocket I had some more money - around 40 or 45 dollars, it might have even been more, I don't know. So I gave him a 20 dollar tip for his kind, hard work throughout the day. Unashamedly he gave me the biggest smile I've ever seen across a man's face, with tears in his eyes.

'Thank you, thank you Mister Sean.'

I could imagine that money I gave him being the equivalent of two or maybe three days' hard work y'know, and it made me feel sick 'cos that to us on board our luxury home in dock was nothing. I must admit that by this time I was holding back the tears with a huge lump coming to my throat, so without hesitation I gave him the rest of what I had in my pocket, gave the guy a hug, knowing I probably wouldn't see him again in my life and headed up the gangway. I'm sure his story is repeated with thousands of people all over his poverty-stricken, but beautiful, ruined city.

All I could hear as I was walking away and for days afterwards was:

Thank you Mister Sean, thank you.

New York – The worlds best

Sydney – I come from a land down under!

St Petersberg – Tis very cold ya!

Mombassa – Safari time

Giza – Me and the Pyramids

Cannes – Fun and frolicking in Cannes

Port Douglas – The barrier reef diver

Saigon – My Saigon taxi

When Bono came to Bath

Bali – The Bali boys

Los Angeles - RIP Marilyn

Los Angeles – Hooray for Hollywood

The Comeback – The lady and her Champ

Acapulco – The fearless divers

Thirteen
Dublin

My book would not be about me had I not put in my experiences of one of my all-time favourite cities in the whole world, Dublin. My love for the place stems from it being the hometown of my favourite rock band, U2. Dublin is to U2 in the same way Liverpool is to The Beatles or Manchester is to Oasis. So I was always intrigued to see what the actual city had to offer after listening to people who had already been there. I was not disappointed. The Irish people all over the city are friendly, hospitable and great for a laugh, and just so laid back it's unreal. If they were any more laid back they'd be falling over!

My first visit to Dublin was back in about 1989, part of a stopover along our journey around Ireland by train on an 'Inter-rail' ticket, a ticket you used to be able to buy that enabled you to travel around the Republic of Ireland and Europe. Due to the fact Dublin was our main interest we always found ourselves back there. But that's not to say we didn't enjoy the other towns and cities of Ireland. In fact, I'll be writing about the city of Cork next to tell you of an amazing guy we met there.

Now you are quite entitled to think that my visits to Dublin were a kind of pilgrimage towards the boys of U2 and part of me would agree but the other part would not because as I've pointed out, the people are great and the scenery and night life are excellent. What more could you want?

But for this chapter I'm going to write about my pilgrimages because the people who know me would expect me to write about them — so I am. During my years of going to Dublin I've been very unlucky. I've sometimes been to the hotel they own and have just missed them. Other days I've been to their local pubs and just missed them. I've been to Bono's house and found out he's out of the country and on other days I've hung around the recording studios to be told that they sneaked out the backdoor because they had to dash off. 'Aaaaaagghhh!'

But my dreams were answered, and I say 'dreams' because if you've got an idol of some sort, whether it be a rock star, movie star or a sporting star that you've followed from a teenager, then it is always your dream to one day meet them.

17th April 1999

My wife at the time, Casey, and I had decided to return to Dublin for our first anniversary. So being huge fans, what better way to celebrate than by booking a table at the Clarence Hotel, owned by U2?

The Tea Room Restaurant there is very beautiful, but very contemporary – stylish but not over the top. We had decided that we were going to enjoy ourselves big time so we supped cocktails at the hotel bar first, very casually, whilst munching on the hors d'oeuvres (it's French for little snacks). After about an hour we were summoned to our table in the restaurant. We didn't care about the expenses so we ordered a lovely bottle of wine to complement our choice of food (I'm talking rather posh right now, aren't I?).

The night was going perfectly – the food, the wine, the service – everything. Halfway through the meal my wife looked over my shoulder and explained to me that behind me sitting at a table was Monica Lewinsky.

'No way,' I replied. So naturally I slowly turned my head in the direction of her table to settle my curiosity, only to find that the lady very much resembled Miss Lewinsky but was not her. As I turned back Casey is laughing at me. 'Ha, ha, ha,' she giggled. 'I'll get you for that,' I promised.

As we eventually finished our main course we kindly asked our waitress if we could have the dessert menu sent up to us in the area at the far end of the restaurant, which is a lounge-come-bar area, with its own little cocktail bar. It is on a raised area that overlooks the whole restaurant, very comfy. Without any problems she agreed to do so once we had left the table. So we both took a relaxing position in our chairs whilst our gourmet food was settling, a chance for us to undo our top buttons, so to speak.

I glance to my right and notice a figure talking to the maître d' in the doorway. To my shock, horror, surprise – whatever you want to call it – it was Bono and his wife Ali. I could feel my face going white and my heart pounding as my wife Casey reached over to ask if I was okay.

'B... B... Bono,' I stuttered.

'Yeah right,' as she started laughing, thinking it was payback time for the 'Lewinsky' joke earlier.

'I'm not kidding — look!'

When she finally realises I'm not joking she gives out a high-pitched, but short-lived scream, so as not to embarrass ourselves. I watch as he walks right by our table... but wait a minute, where is he sitting?

Oh my God, he's gone up the small stairs to the raised area where we have ordered our desserts to be sent to, and he's only gone and sat at the table next to ours that has already been set up for us! Oh my God!

Finally realising that you have the opportunity to meet your idol – the man you have listened to and watched on video and television, the man you have searched for on previous trips and have watched live on stage – is a nerve-wracking experience, let me tell you. Even at 31-years-old I was a shaking mess! When we both got up to make our way to our table I thought I was going drop to the floor, I couldn't control my knocking knees. I remember Casey saying to me, 'Just relax, take it easy.'

I managed to pull myself together eventually, as we walked up the stairs to our desserts.

Getting to our table seemed to take an eternity so when we did get there, after catching our breath, I sent Casey over first 'cos I was still a nervous wreck. She was so cool about it as well. She went over to his table which was only about two yards away and introduced herself. At that point I was unable to see him anymore until he leaned back in his chair and said, 'Good evening' to me. That was my cue for movement towards his table.

'Good evening Bono how ya doing?' I said as I firmly shook his hand. We sat there with him and his wife, during which time I told him it was an absolute pleasure to finally meet him and thanked him for the lyrics to my life. I couldn't help but charm his wife because besides being very beautiful she was also six months pregnant at the time, giving a radiant glow.

One of the things that really impressed me about meeting Bono was the fact that he didn't ignore or brush us off like a lot of stars might have, y'know.

Instead he actually made conversation with us, asked us about our trip and congratulated us on our anniversary. He was even good enough to sign our dessert menu:

Congratulations Sean and Casey Bono '99

Fan-bloody-tastic! If he'd 'ave ignored us I think I would have been crushed, devastated, but he showed us respect and was patient with us. In return we didn't overstay our welcome, so we said or 'goodbyes' and 'thank-you's' and went back to our table because the guy probably gets stopped all the time. My respect for the man grew even bigger than it was beforehand. But it's amazing, all the time that I'd been trying to catch up with him I always thought I knew what I'd say to him but, in reality I was dumbstruck! And I never did get to say everything I wanted.

Anyway, as we sat there trying to take it all in, our desserts had melted to a flimsy mess – which, to be honest, was the last thing on my mind. So we ordered a bottle of champagne to celebrate our anniversary and our chance meeting.

To top the night off, for Casey especially, as the maître 'd came to him to inform him that his table was ready, Bono came over to us, shook my hand again and then grabbed Casey by the arm and give her a kiss and a cuddle and said 'Congratulations' again. This time she was dumbstruck and speechless, whilst I give Ali another kiss and wished her good health with the baby. After he left for his table I don't think Casey and me spoke for another ten or fifteen minutes – we were both blown away.

'More champagne please,' I asked.

So the pair of us just sat there chilling out with the occasional glance at his table just to make sure it was him. I've met the man a few times since but nothing can ever top that first meeting. What was all the more surprising was while on another visit to Dublin about two years later (during which time me and Casey had split up), I got to meeting him again. As I approached him outside their recording studios he glanced at me with a curious look.

'Have we met before?' he asked.

'Yes,' I said, 'About two years ago at the Tea Room.'

'Oh yeah, I remember, you were with your wife right?'

'Yes I was,' I replied.

With that reply I watched him go back into his head and rummage around his memory bank to bring out the name: 'Casey, your wife's name, it was Casey yeah?' From stunned silence I replied, 'Yes it was, how the hell did you remember that, that was two years ago?'

The man coolly put his arm around me as we posed for a picture and replied, 'I never forget a name.' Even though we're not together anymore, that signed dessert menu to me and Casey hangs proudly in my office at home.

Wow... the man is a god.

Fourteen
Cork

During my time of travelling, certain people have had special reasons to remain in my memory, people like Simon Hale and Father Peter whom I mentioned in my Hong Kong chapter, or the guy in Saigon who give me a bike ride around the city, or my first taxi-driver in New York. I met another guy on my travels in Ireland that I would have such a lasting memory of.

It was during my inter-rail trip around Ireland with my French girlfriend I had at the time, Valerie, that our trip was taking us to Cork. We had been told it was a great place for fun and a few beers. I think we were travelling from Limerick by train, which was going to take us at least two hours. So we armed ourselves with our cans and our Walkman that had little speakers to plug in, and away we went.

Being typical backpackers we weren't fully prepared, because halfway through the journey our Walkman started to pack up on us and we had no alternative to the music. In the seat behind Valerie I could see this young guy listening in to our problem, so I asked him if he knew how to fix our music. In a typical rough Irish accent he replied, 'Yes.' 'So come and join us,' I suggested, and without hesitation he climbed over and began to explain that he worked in a Currys outlet in the city centre.

While he was taking the Walkman apart we introduced ourselves as Sean and Val, and in return he replied, 'I'm Seamus, pleased ta meetchya.'

After about 15 minutes he had the music back on and we were getting on well, drinking our cans of cider together, chatting away. He was asking us where we were due to stay upon our arrival in Cork, which at that time we didn't really know ourselves. So he suggested getting into his car, which was parked at the station, and he would take us to a hostel where he knew the people who worked there, and would look after us really well for a good price.

By this time I was getting a bit suspicious of our Seamus, so I was trying to put him off. Well you know you can't be too naïve about these things can you? I mean we'd only just met him, now here he was offering us a lift around town to a hostel we didn't know anything about. I could just picture a group of his mates at the station waiting for us, or him having us over for all our money and our passports. But I remember Val was getting a bit pissed by now, so she was insisting on going along with everything he suggested. It wasn't until he got up to go to the men's room that I had a chance to speak to her properly, after which she realised what I was trying to say. I mean I wasn't turning the guy down, it's just that I was being careful y'know. But while we were together on the train we were best mates and we still had a few cans to finish.

Cork station finally arrived and we agreed to take him up on his offer with one eye over my shoulder. True enough his car was there and off we went towards the city centre. Along the way he was pointing out the best places for a pint or two later. Later, what's he talking about?

We finally arrived at the hostel he was telling us about. He jumped out first and ran up the steps to the main reception area. A few minutes later he came out to tell us there were rooms available. What's this guy up to I was wondering, people aren't usually this friendly with strangers. Or is it different here in Ireland? I was beginning to think it was because we were in Ireland and he was a genuine good guy. I mean he couldn't do enough for us. He even carried Val's backpack and offered to carry mine too.

So we checked into this hostel and gave a big 'Thank you' to Seamus. But his hospitality didn't stop there. As we were shaking hands he suggested that he come back later to take us into town and have a night out with him. I must admit I was beginning to take to this guy, not 100%, but I was relaxing with him. So we agreed a time for him to come back for us. A couple of hours later after a shag and a shower we were ready, as was Seamus – and on time as well.

The city centre of Cork was full of people of all ages enjoying themselves – there was a real good buzz about the place. By this time I was totally relaxed with the situation and we were all having a great time. During one of many visits to the ladies by Val, Seamus was good enough to come to me and talk about my reluctance to trust him at first and could totally understand my suspicions. But he couldn't stress the point enough that he was a genuine good guy and just wanted to help because he appreciated the conversation and the cider cans on the train. So for the rest of the night I was at ease and the beers flowed. And for last orders he even took us to his local pub to introduce us to the landlord. As a result the landlord shouted that any friend of Seamus was a friend of his, then closed the doors for a lock-in. The drinks came thick and fast from every direction. His bunch of mates were just as friendly as he was, and if Val wasn't there I could have got off with some of his female ones too – they were loving my northern accent.

By the end of the night we were totally smashed – every one of us in the place. It was great. How on earth Seamus drove us back without crashing I'll never know to this day. Needless to say, we had mighty hangovers the next day!

The following day Val and I walked around the city doing the tourist things before phoning Seamus to come and meet us for some lunch to say 'Thank you'. The rest of the story is a bit of a blur because of the large amounts of alcohol consumed, because I can't remember if we ever did meet up with him or not, or whether we just spoke on the phone.

But what I can remember is that meeting up with Seamus was one of the highlights of that trip and it was a real pleasure knowing the guy, even if it was for just one night. He did more for Ireland that day and night then any tourist board could ever do. I've always had that memory of him like I do with Father Peter, Simon and everyone else like them who left a large impression upon me.

Seamus... fair play to ya.

Fifteen
Bali

During one of my contracts on board the *Song of Flower*, the ship had to go in for its annual 'dry dock' period which can be up to ten or eleven days. It's like a car going in for its MOT, only on a bigger scale. This was to take place in Singapore.

Once again the captain and the hotman sat down together, and because they didn't need all the crew present they decided that the crew members who had completed at least half of their six month contract could take nine days leave. The other half of the crew had to stay on board to scrub and clean, and live in dirty conditions whilst everything, and I mean everything, was changed or repaired. One of the crew who had to stay was my Swedish girlfriend Anna. Awww... unlucky!

Some friends and I decided to take advantage of this generous offer and head off to Bali for a break. We had actually been there before so the choice of vacation wasn't too difficult. The group of us who went really did our best for 'United Nations'. We had with us an Italian guy named Andrea, a Dutch guy named Eugene, a German guy named Fredrick and two Scottish girls by the name of Karen and Liz, and me, a Geordie. 'Bali 'ere we come!'

Funny thing was though, when we got there it was absolutely pissing it down! Typical eh! Walking distance from the plane to the terminal was quite a trot so naturally we got soaking wet by the time we reached the building. It was just your typical everyday rainstorm, the locals kept saying. It didn't last too long, and after about 20 minutes the clouds opened up and out came the beautiful sunshine accompanied by the heat.

We went straight to the tourist desk to sort out the accommodation, then it was off sorting out the transportation. Surprise surprise, right outside was a fleet of cars with each of the drivers shouting and begging for our business. Some of them were really pushy and annoying – all except this one guy who was stood alone at the end of the line just leaning against his Volkswagen van reading his newspaper, as if to say 'I'm not getting involved in all that.'

Something just mentally clicked between us all as we found ourselves walking towards this guy.

'Hey, you,' we shouted. He looked up at us as if to say, 'Who, me?'

'How much to take us to Kuta Beach Cottages?' The other drivers couldn't believe it as we walked straight past them, they were gob-smacked.

The guy finally stuttered out a price and off we went. He never once made eye contact with the other drivers as he got into the van from his side, it was very amusing. But as soon as we left the airport grounds we couldn't get him to stop chatting, he was so talkative. A real nice guy though. A few minutes later we finally reached our accommodation, which were beautiful little individual cottages, with tiled floors, old oak beams overhead, two single beds and a huge shower room. In the grounds we had two swimming pools, two restaurants (one of which was open 24 hours) and a bar that was also 24 hours. And boy were we going to get a lot of use out of the facilities!

While we were in the van we had quietly agreed to hire this guy for the whole time we were here in Bali. So when it came to asking him if he was available, he couldn't believe it, his face was a picture. 'Yes, yes!' was his quick reply.

We told him that we would pay him very generously if he were here at our request day or night to take us anywhere we wished. You could literally see the dollar signs in his eyes ticking over. Our guy's name was Sam. He was a short guy with a little chubby figure, slightly balding and with three teeth missing from his top row, but he was a real gem of a man. And sure enough, whenever we wanted him he was there on time and he took us all over the island. We even had him take us to other bars and clubs on the other side of the island too. All the time we were inside a bar or club Sam would just park up somewhere and go to sleep. Some nights we weren't getting back 'till four or five in the morning, then up in a couple of hours to be taken to the beaches, unless they were walking distance.

One morning we woke up after the night before and Eugene was feeling a little delicate, to say the least. We had planned to go surfing, all except Eugene that is, so he came along just to chill out in the sun. From the cottages to the beach was about a ten minute walk, but to him it must of felt like ten miles 'cos by the time we got there he was sweating buckets. No sooner had we suggested that he take a seat, he just keeled over face down into the sand with no arms out to break his fall – just flat bang, out like a light. It was the funniest thing! We quickly picked him up (how I don't know 'cos we were in fits of laughter) and placed him under a tree for the shade. Along various spots of the beach you have these old women offering you a massage for a cheap price. Well, someone from this women's group must have noticed Eugene's condition so they came over to help. Between us guys we arranged for these women to look after him with a massage, lots of water and lots of TLC. He was starting to come around as we left for the ocean. Soon he realised he was in his own little heaven, even though they were rather old and wrinkly.

On another day we decided to distance ourselves from the two girls, as they wanted to go in one direction and us boys in the other, so we said our 'see ya later,' and headed off. In between a few pit-stops involving the local beverage houses, we were approached by a group of beautiful young Balinese ladies who wanted us to sit with them while they plaited our hair with colourful beads. Being typical males on holiday we fell for their charms so agreed to accompany them.

They sat us in a row along the top of some steps while they did their plaiting business, even supplying us with cold bottles of coke. Because we were sat along these steps it was sometimes difficult for local people to get by so they had to brush alongside of us to get past. On a couple of occasions the four of us would receive what we call a 'twister' (a twisting of the skin using your fingers) on our shoulders, as the local girls struggled to walk past us, but it was always greeted with laughter from the girls doing our hair.

We naturally thought that we were upsetting these people by making them climb past us to get by, but we didn't think much of it – a bit rude, but not too worrying. It was only when Eugene received an almighty twister from one girl that he decided enough was enough, so he made a loud abusive remark back in the direction of this young lady. Once again it was greeted with laughter from our hairstylists.

'What's going on with these people?' Eugene asked.

'The ladies are admiring you sir, they think you handsome,' replied a pretty voice behind us.

'It old tradition for Balinese women to pinch you if she like you,' she explained.

'Ahhh... okay. We like that one,' we all answered.

So for the next ten minutes or so we were gratefully accepting these twisters knowing the meaning behind them was encouraging – that is up until the time I received the mother of all twisters. The pain was enormous. I thought, 'What the hell,' and the other guys were in fits of laughter while I was feverishly rubbing my stinging shoulder. It wasn't until I turned to face the culprit that I discovered why the laughter... it was a man!

He was standing there gazing so lovingly at me while he gave me a little wave then carried on walking. 'Ahhhhhh... why me?!'

This even made our lady friends behind us laugh out loud as well. So you can imagine the stick I took for the rest of the day as we walked the streets wearing our hair in 'Rasta' coloured beads.

It was on another trip to Bali that I first experienced white-water rafting, and what great fun it is as well, I can assure you. One big adrenaline rush if you're into that sort of thing, as I am. The water is bloody cold but the speeds you can pick up are amazing and the whites of the water come racing at you with crashing sounds. And the fear reaches boiling point as you approach your first drop in the water. You're instructed to paddle 'till the last possible moment then cling onto the handles situated around your dingy as you go over the edge.

The screams of delight as you come up out of the water are those of an American on Super Bowl day with a touchdown in the last minute of the game. But then you've got to paddle like crazy so as not to get sucked under with the current – that's when the tops of your arms really start to feel the hard work going in to it. Once you've accomplished that it's relax time until the next one, that's when the American in you starts shouting out again, 'Wooooo... alright!'

I would truly recommend Bali as a port to stop off at during your trips. Look out for the Kuta Cottages and a taxi driver called Sam. You can't miss him, small and chubby, balding and three teeth missing along his top row – tell him Mr Sean says hello.

All these nights out and long lazy days in the sun all served as good holiday memories for us all. That was a truly great week in Bali, a holiday I've never forgotten. Oh and at the end of the week we paid Sam $50 each, which he was more than happy with as he gave us a big huge hug and smile. I'll never forget that toothless guy. By the time we got back to the ship we still had two days to enjoy in Singapore. And I had my Anna waiting for me – I think she missed me! And a stay in Singapore isn't complete without going to the famous Raffles Hotel for their well-known Singapore Slings.

Hic!

Sixteen
Corfu

The Greek Island of Corfu – great place but unfortunately it's my 'unlucky' island! On two occasions I've cheated death and received a written warning.

Really?

Yes really.

Well doesn't that make it your lucky island then?

I guess so in a way, but I've been unlucky in crashing a scooter and then a jeep on separate visits.

Ah... okay.

Corfu is a colourful place full of colourful people, so when you go there you can't help but want to enjoy yourself. And right outside the port gates are the perfect boys' toys:

'Motorbikes and scooters for hire... very cheap.'

And to be the macho boy you're not required to wear a helmet either. Wicked!

Now think back to the earlier chapter when I said I was the 'thrill seeker' on the fast bikes. Can you imagine me wearing a helmet when I didn't have to? I think not. So there I was on my powerful scooter (well I can't ride the motor bikes but hey, Dennis Hopper learnt to ride on a scooter before he did *Easy Rider*), with my Swedish Anna on the bike behind, hitting the speed limits. We were demons of speed!

After we had dodged our way round the city centre with me forgetting that the locals drove on the other side, we decided to stop for a few beers and something to eat at the top of this hillside. We were there for about two hours when we decided to leave. As we both pulled away from this café heading downhill and picking up speed, Anna had overtaken me and was about ten yards in front of me when my back wheel skidded on something, sending me all over the place. Keeping my speed going once I'd controlled the bike I glanced down at the road to see what could have been responsible, not noticing that Anna had slowed down to see what my problem was. As I looked up to face the road she was about three yards in front of me and I was still flying along at speed!

'Shit!' was my response. I quickly managed to avoid her, just, but now I was heading towards the little three foot wall separating the road and the drop on the other side.

'Oh shit,' was my next comment. Squeezing hard on my brakes, I still hit the wall with a big thud, sending the back of the bike upwards like a backward 'wheelie' that almost sent me over the handlebars. I could see the drop becoming more visible to me as I was forced closer to it, knowing that I still had this bloody bike attached to my arse. By this time I think I burnt holes in my trainers as I tried to use them as extra brakes. It always reminds me of the Flintstones when I think back to how they used to stop their cars.

Luckily the back wheel meets earth again with a sudden drop and I was okay. Besides hitting my shins on the stone wall, the damage to the bike was 'hide-able' with a few tugs here and there. The chap at the bike office didn't notice, so we got out deposit back. Phew!

The laughter immediately afterwards was a nervous one, but once we were on ship and in the crew bar later that evening, the laughter turned into a piss-take, but I didn't mind Anna as she was taking care of my bruises using her Swedish methods.

We'd gone back to Corfu the day before my birthday during a sunny August, so me and my best mate Keith had decided to have a cabin party. As I said earlier about the colourful place Corfu, just along from the bike hire place is an even better boys' toy shop: an English off-licence!

So we took a casual stroll along to the establishment, as you do when it's your birthday, returning with a shopping trolley with large amounts of alcohol. The contents were quickly placed in our fridge, and then it was off to meet our dates for the day, Sweet Mary and Sexy Julia from the dancing trio. It was decided that because I'd crashed the scooter a few weeks before that, this time we'd hire an open top jeep — fantastic!

Towels, shades, sun lotion, music box and a couple of beers, and we were off to find some deserted beach on the other side of the island all to ourselves. Going at top speeds around the winding roads with the wind in our faces, music blaring away, was just what we all needed after we'd just had one of those cruises from hell that was busy, busy with crazy difficult people. So there we were, girls in the back, sunshine beaming down on us and no duties until 6.30 that night and Keith was driving. We spotted the beach that was perfect for us, so for the whole afternoon we chilled out while taking the occasional dip to cool us off.

Sadly the day was coming to an end so we had to head back to allow ourselves plenty of time to settle up with the jeep's deposit and have a shit, shave and shower before work. Keith was doing his usual speeds as we approached a long stretch of road with a left turn at the end of it. Suddenly from around the corner came a Ford Cortina - only he was on the same side as us. Keith being English along with the two girls didn't realise our mistake - we were the ones on the wrong side of the bloody road!

Me and Keith glanced at each other. Shhhit!

Then with an extremely loud screech of the brakes we met the Cortina head on with a crash bang, then nowt but silence.

A few seconds passed before we raised our heads to examine ourselves. 'I'm okay' was the response from everyone, everyone except me. I couldn't feel my legs and I had a trickle of blood coming down my forehead. Yeah I know, I should have had my seat belt on! On impact I'd slid down my seat and hit the crash bars under the dash board with my knees, then head-butted the windscreen a beauty.

The driver of the other car got out and was okay, just a little shaken up, and although it was our mistake he was very concerned and immediately got on to his mobile to call an ambulance. During the time it took for the ambulance to arrive I remained in my seat unable to move while we were listening to this man in broken English describe our 'blow out, blow out.'

What's he talking about - we've just smashed into his car because we were driving on the wrong side of the road - there was no 'blow out' with our tyres. Suddenly it clicked with me and Keith that we could use this guy to make a statement for us to the hire company so that we didn't get charged with the costs of repairing the jeep.

'Okay, okay, yeah, it was a blow out,' we agreed.

We couldn't figure what this guy was on but hey, if it saved our arses then we'd go along with it. The ambulance finally turned up and I was lifted out to reveal two huge swollen knees. It was then I could see the extent of the damage with both cars looking like one, as they were mashed into each other, twisted and broken beyond repair. Somebody was looking out for me that day.

Keith was dropped off outside the hire company's office, along with the fella in the other car, and I along with the girls was dropped off at the ship's gangway with a wheelchair waiting for me. After spending about an hour in the medical room, Keith and the girls came along to tell me that we had got away without paying a penny, so between the four of us we gave out huge laughter and said we should do it again sometime! Unbelievable, eh?

After being strapped up and wiped clean I was sent to my cabin where I was to remain in bed resting... yeah right, I still had a party to have that evening, remember. I made a decision at the beginning of this book not to have too many stories of my drunken behaviour because you've heard it all before I'm sure, but this evening's party needs to be told.

So there I am strapped up, with the crutches by my bedside, receiving all the TLC attention from the females in attendance – it was great. The party started getting loud and messy with everyone finishing their shift upstairs, but we were running out of room for them all. Keith had the bright idea to have it in the crew mess, only I wasn't allowed out of my cabin remember. It took only a few minutes to persuade me to struggle on down to the mess once everything had been transferred there. The party carried on in full swing with everyone getting seriously drunk, including me! It's taken years of practice but you learn to carry on regardless of your difficulties. After all, it was my birthday don't forget.

I somehow made it back to my bed later that night to be woken up the next morning with Keith shouting at me to get ready because the hotman wanted to see us both. 'Why?' I asked.

We eventually made it up the stairs to his office where he wiped the floor with us both and then proceeded to give us both written warnings. He explained because I was off duty due to the injuries I had received, I should not have left my cabin, and he gave Keith one just for the hell of it I think. We left his office with our ears burning and a smirk on our faces as we passed everyone involved in the night's celebrations listening outside.

I went back to bed to nurse my hangover, while Keith went back to laying up the whole restaurant on his own for lunch as punishment. There was talk of me being sent home because of my injuries, but the healing powers of booze, pain killers and the threat of returning home and missing out on all the fun are amazing. I still suffer some pain in my knees today but I sit and suffer, and think back to the fun we had, and say to myself, 'It was bloody worth it.'

But I'm in no rush to return to Corfu, my unlucky island.

Seventeen
Los Angeles

I've thought long and hard about whether or not to put this chapter in my book, mostly because I'm not with the lady in question anymore and it's been one hell of an emotional roller coaster. But LA does have its good stories to tell, which is the whole point of me writing my chronicles, so I've thought well, why not? And besides, how many other guys can claim to have a better story than me when it comes to proposing to their girlfriends?

Throughout my whole travelling life I've experienced highs and lows during my adventures, but my greatest high reached 'Everest' heights when I first laid eyes on a beautiful Californian girl from Pasadena by the name of Casey. 'Wow, she's gorgeous,' I thought to myself.

I first remember seeing her when I worked on board the *Crystal Symphony*. At the time I was working in the night club bar when she came in with her dancer friends for a boogie and some cocktails. I know she doesn't remember meeting me, but I thought to myself, 'If I could have any woman on my arm to love and be proud of that would be her.' She had a fun personality, big beautiful eyes, lovely brown hair, a huge smile, confidence, and she oozed sex appeal with her slim body. She paid little attention to me at the time though, just a polite 'thank you' as I poured more Chardonnay or mixed her a few more Cosmopolitans. I was to find out later from the other bartenders that she was a frequent visitor to the ship due to the fact that from her LA office ashore she controlled the sales ladies on board, who were selling the ship to passengers wanting to come back for a future voyage, so I was confident our paths would meet again. And they did during the last ten-day cruise of my six-month contract. There is a God!

She was on board at this time with her parents, who were celebrating a wedding anniversary, so it took me a long time to actually get talking to her (plus I had to find the courage), but when we did we hit it off like a house on fire – she was everything I hoped she'd be and more. We were totally smitten with each other and promised to keep in touch. She got off at San Pedro, which is the port for Los Angeles and I got off two days later in San Francisco. After endless and extremely long phone calls to each other, plus her jumping on a plane to Heathrow a couple of times with me there waiting, we had decided we were right for each other, so she went home to quit her job and to move out to England. We couldn't get enough of each other!

We had been corresponding with immigration and discovered that for Casey to live and work in the UK legally she would have to have a fiancée visa. We'd been giving it some serious thought so I went out and bought an engagement ring.

The days couldn't go by quick enough before I was on that plane ready for my three week trip to LA with the prospect of returning with the girl of my dreams, plus I had a proposal to plan out as well.

One of the common bonds that we discovered about each other during our first meetings was our admiration and liking of a Hollywood legend... Marilyn Monroe. Casey went on to explain how she had had a fascination with her since she was a kid, and had collected her books and knew the whole history of the lady, as well as having the pleasure of paying her respects at her graveside and also visiting the house she had died in. So to be included in the tourist trips Casey was taking me on during the first days I was there, I asked for Marilyn's graveside to be amongst the sights.

The day came towards the end of the stay and we had a planned visit to immigration later that same afternoon.

We drove to the Burbank area of Century City in LA to pay homage to our female hero in glorious sunshine and I knew the moment was right. Driving between the skyscrapers you could easily miss the cemetery if you didn't know it was there, it's so secluded in between all the traffic noise and concrete, so much so that people in the nearby offices go there for their lunch hour to enjoy the peacefulness of the place.

As I entered the area the one thing that struck me was that it didn't look like a graveyard as such, it looked more like a quiet park. I mean, the grass wasn't covered in your typical old, falling down, covered-in-weed crosses or the dirty headstones out of a horror movie.

The lawns were beautifully manicured and the deceased were marked with bronze plaques with remembrance words inscribed – the most famous I recognised lying there was Natalie Wood. As you walk over to the far right of the cemetery the walls are made of beautiful white marble with crypts placed four high, with a bronze plaque in the centre of each individual three feet by three feet marble front inscribed with the name of the person and their dates.

As Casey walked me towards her all I could think about was, 'Wow, there she is.' We finally stood there in front of her, on the other side of the wall of course. And so for the next two or three minutes we didn't speak a word to each other, just stood and stared. The final resting place of the most famous lady in the movie industry. Wow.

Then it hit me: this is it, right here, right now... how strangely romantic. I sat Casey down on the marble bench dedicated to Marilyn, got down on one knee and told her much I loved her and how much I would love to marry her, as I showed her the ring I'd been carrying around in my pocket for days, waiting for the right moment.

To my pleasure she said yes straight away so we gave each other a huge kiss and hug and thanked Marilyn for being present, as we could both imagine her sat above us somewhere, supping a Martini with a little tear rolling down her cheek and into her chilled drink. Now isn't that (strangely) romantic eh?

I like to use my imagination and be different sometimes, so I carried the ring around for days just waiting for that spontaneous, somewhere different moment to come along and there it was, in a graveyard in LA the home of Hollywood! Ha, ha, ha!

I still get a chuckle out of it today when I think of it. How many people can say that they got engaged in a graveyard eh?

Casey enjoyed it and she had a tear in her eye and agreed it was a very appropriate place. We didn't care that the rest of the afternoon was spent in an immigration office filling in forms, we were going to be together forever, well... three-and-a-half years anyway.

I thought I'd found what I was looking for, in the City of Angels.

Eighteen
The Comeback – My Greatest Achievement

I'm sat in front of my laptop contemplating whether to include this amongst my chapters, only because it takes a little detour away from my tales of swashbuckling adventures upon the high seas. But then I got to thinking that it's without doubt what I class as my greatest achievement bar none, and I want to share it with you all, so while a sharp cutlass directs me along the plank take a breather while I take a dip!

Ever since I retired from my fighting days back in my late teens I have never lost the love and passion for the sport of boxing. Way before Sky Sports and pay-per-view hit our LCD/plasma surround-sound all mod-con telly, I remember fondly listening to the big fights on my little black non-DAB radio. For me the fight between Hagler and Hearns, dubbed 'The War', was one of the greatest; the biggest one for shocks was the Honeyghan versus Curry fight, which in a way I'm glad was enjoyed on my radio, because it provided fantastic memories of how things were back then, 20 years plus.

Once you've experienced the excitement and flow of adrenalin come the time your trainer says to you, 'It's time kid,' it's very difficult to leave go of it. I know a lot of ex-fighters out there reading this will agree with me. Although I've always kept myself fit since my fighting days, my years away from the ring and the gym surroundings have been spent in the posing palaces full of those grunting over-muscled prima donnas called fitness gyms. I was travelling with work a lot, both home and abroad, and these gyms were provided with the job. I've never felt comfortable with them but used them anyway just to stay reasonably fit – but for me you can't beat the sweaty smells and sounds of a boxing gym. The pounding of the heavy bag, the clipping sounds of the skipping ropes on the hard floor to the bass lines of some awful dance music and the favourite of mine, the speed ball. They say you never forget your first shag or your first family holiday and for many fighters those rhythmic sounds I've described never leave you either.

I remember those first steps going upstairs with my dad, feeling nervous as hell but excited at the same time to my first proper gym that was situated above a pub (the best ones always are) in my home town of Stockton-on-Tees. We were quite fortunate in our town for having three gyms to choose from: we had two amateur and one professional club. My dad had a work mate who was a pro, who was happy to take me under his wing and introduce me to his world. The club was run by an ex-pro by the name of Maxi Smith (I'm sure some of you boxing historians will have heard of him) who in his day was a top ten light heavyweight of the '70the s and fought Bunny Stirling. He was due to fight John Conteh for the Commonwealth title until the popular scouser pulled out with injury.

I loved watching the pros doing their workout overlooked by the familiar faces of the past great eras, immortalised in cracked picture frames: Ali, Duran, Dempsey, Hagler, Louis, Hearns, the all-time greats being protected from the draft by the fight posters covering the gaps in the walls. The place was a wreck and bloody cold but I loved it and started the very next night raring to go and eager to learn. I was fourteen.

The gym lingo and obscenities coming from Max's lips were embedded into my head from an early age: 'push yourself', 'jab and move', 'last ten' and the painful 'one more'! To everyone who's ever entered a boxing ring, whether it be in Manchester or Madison, to London or Las Vegas, those words ring familiar to us all. It's often said that boxing is all about two blokes belting hell out of each other. Well they couldn't be further from the truth if they tried. That's the kind of scene you might, sorry you will, see out on a Saturday night. Within the gym walls you're taught discipline, self-control, respect for yourself and others, from which you will gain friendship and camaraderie of your fellow contenders. Each hard session of blood, sweat and tears always ended with a wink of approval or a tap of the gloves, even though you've thrown solid combinations and bloodied each other's nose. Every night ended in a laugh and joke – not a hint of malice or bad-tempered egos.

It was that kind of atmosphere that I always missed and longed to rediscover someday, even if the years were passing me by. In February 2008 I found my belonging and I'll talk more about that a bit later, but for now I'd like to reminisce about my younger fighting days travelling up and down the country with my new trainer who by this time had changed.

After I served my apprenticeship under my first guru Maxi, I was encouraged to join one of the amateur clubs in town, the most popular being run by a well-known man on the local circuit by the name of Sid Hogg, who with his wife Marion used to run Stockton Amateur Boxing Club. This purpose-built gym given to them by the council was fantastic: it had changing rooms, showers, toilets, a kitchen and a storage room/office. Although I loved my first gym this was bliss compared to the damp freezing cold place I'd been learning my novice skills from.

Marion would look after us boys like we were her own: she'd monitor our weight, take our gym fees, arrange medicals with the local health centres and organise the match-making over the phone with other clubs up and down the country. This was well before the Internet was around. I even remember she sometimes provided a towel for you so you could have a shower! We were on the road every other week travelling to Scotland, Wales, north, south, east and west of the UK. We even sent boxers to Denmark to represent a northeast select English team (myself included in the light welterweight division). This left the gym work to Sid who was a great man, of whom I have fond memories and great respect for. His enthusiasm, knowledge, sense of humour and fitness for a man of his age was amazing to see from a lad of my tender age of sixteen. Although the training was hard and there were plenty of times being physically sick with the punishment my body was taking, he always had a way of making us enjoy it and taking our minds away from the pain. To me this was a key to a having a successful stable of young boxers who enjoyed what they were doing. The endless sit-ups, the pads, the skipping, the bag work, shadow boxing, the long hours doing roadwork and then the hard sparring sessions all accounted for the crop of winners we had amongst us. We had a Featherweight ABA winner in Mohammed Haniff and kids who won national schoolboy titles. Amongst them was a young Geoff McCreesh who in the pro ranks won the British Welterweight title, beating Kevin Leushing on an emotional night, just days after his father had died. During his days as an amateur he was a vicious little buggar to spar, but you could see he had that 'championship' quality about him. I for one was in tears the night he won his title. Stockton Amateur Boxing Club was the place to be!

They were a fantastic partnership Sid and Marion, and I'd like to take this opportunity to thank them for everything they did for me and the rest of the lads. We we were one big family and I loved every minute of it. My own personal fight record was a modest 19 fights: won three, lost 16 – which might suggest why I was overlooked by Frank Warren when the world titles were up for grabs – but I was pleased with my efforts considering I boxed away from home a lot of the time and felt rather aggrieved with one or three of the decisions going against me, one of which was the trip to Denmark. The old quote from Henry Cooper comes to mind when he says, 'When you box in Europe you have to knock 'em out to win on points.' This was very true in my case.

Anyway, I won my first three fights all by stoppage and was on a real high when I was asked if I fancied boxing a guy from Hartlepool Catholic Boys Club with a record of 11&0 (eleven fights, no defeats, for those with no knowledge!). I was very confident (and dumb) and said yes. Chris Hubbard was his name. After a real good warm up on the pads with Sid we were called to go, which was the first opportunity I got to see Chris as we all walked downstairs to the function room of a big social club. My over-riding memory of that moment was 'fucking hell, he's massive'. I kid you not dear reader, he stood at least 6 feet 4 inches compared to my 5 feet 9. I did manage to make him fight my kind of fight on the inside instead of letting him box my nose off, but the result was inevitable. After a real good toe-to-toe battle for the first two rounds he stopped me mid-way through the last round. It was my first loss and I was devastated. It was made worse because my family and friends were attending for the first time. It took me a long time to get over that loss, maybe longer than I thought. I affected me deep down, sub-consciously. I trained and fought on regardless, searching for that win that would get me back on track, but as hard as I tried it never came, it just never came!

Now, looking back on things I can be honest with myself and say that on some occasions I didn't give it my all, but by then my heart started to wander and my confidence was falling as quick as a demolished tower block. I tried to work hard during the fight — why weren't the judges seeing that? I took some shots but gave plenty back, I had a good jab and good footwork, and it's not as if I was ever in any punishing fights besides that first defeat - but I was feeling angry and disillusioned after every fight, angry with every judge sat at the ring side. If you ever start questioning yourself about your involvement in boxing, together with a lack of confidence, then it's not the sport to be in. It's hard enough as it is without the extra pressures, so I thought it was time to quit, so I did.

Fast forward 22 years, several pounds heavier (I could never make the welterweight division now), I'm giving it another go at the golden age of 40 - wiser and with several years of experience is the way I look at it. The bitterness has all but gone but I've still got 22 years of frustration to wipe away and make amends for, which is why I've set out on this comeback that I think Big George Foreman would be proud of. They say you have to be mad to be a goalkeeper on the football fields, so what would they say about a 40-year-old ex-fighter ready to lace up the gloves again. Oh, by the way, I still play Sunday morning football as well — guess what position? Goalkeeper!

As I'm walking through the streets of Bath one night I notice a fight poster advertising an up-and-coming White Collar Boxing event at the local pavilion. I call the number at the bottom of the poster to enquire about this 'White Collar' titled poster and speak with a guy by the name of Mark Kent (no relation to Clark), who tells me he runs a gym by the name of Ringside in Trowbridge for people of all ages who always wanted to try stepping into the competitive ring. Some would try it just the once, others would box again on the white collar circuit, fighting against guys from a similar novice position. For me that was the spark that got the fire in my belly started - this was an opportunity for someone of my age to end my fighting record on a win. I went along to the night of boxing and from what I saw felt confident my skills and experience would bring me through. I would discover that the white collar gyms are filled with ex-amateur and pro fighters, mostly coaching, or some trying to rekindle their fighting days as I was, although because they've grown too old for the pro and amateur game they do it through the white collar circuit. I didn't care, I just wanted to train and have that one last chance to put things right for myself. I went to Trowbridge on a scouting mission to see how things were run and it was no different from any other gym I'd been to, so I introduced myself to Mark, told him what I wanted to achieve, and he was more than happy to help. We made arrangements for me to start the next session and things started from there really.

As I said earlier about being committed to boxing, this is something I'm not taking lightly, so I've decided to put my whole heart into it. My training nights are Monday, Wednesday and Fridays. They begin with the usual warm-up routines – getting through them is the easy bit, it's the gruesome training that follows which hurts the most, although I must admit that I did feel one or two tweaks as I stretched out! I've no need to describe what every fighter goes through as I'm sure most of my readers already know, but boy oh boy, did I find those first few sessions bloody hard – my body hurt big time!

I recall my first night's controlled sparring and walking onto a peach of a left jab right on the end of my nose! The eyes filled up and the claret flowed freely, and the memories came flooding back all within that flash second. I can say it with a smile on my face now, but it did make me wonder what the hell I was thinking of. The doubt only spurred me on to get things fitter and sharper before I lost the shape of my pretty nose. In fact, it was probably the best thing that could have happened because it woke up my senses and made it all the more real. Even now as I'm writing, I still feel a big grin come across my face when recalling those early sessions.

The fitness had come on a treat and I was really pleased with my progress. The sharpness had returned and the power had never left me. In addition, the confidence that I wasn't making a twat of myself was there too. Being back amongst the 'buzz' was a real pleasure and after five months of hard training I felt accepted and respected within the team of guys down at the gym. As any fighter will tell you, walking into a new gym with new fighters doesn't guarantee you respect from the other guys. You have to earn it the hard way –through the ropes, taking shots and drawing blood and sweat from someone who wants to be the first to kick the butt of the new guy! You have to be prepared to take the knocks and dish it out yourself too – if I wasn't, this comeback fight was gonna be a huge mistake. Showing commitment, heart and determination gets you a long way within the boxing fraternity, and this gym wasn't any different. I've left there with my body aching, my eyes bruised and the dried blood still in my nostrils, but I'd like to think that I've left someone else feeling that way as I've made my way home on the late train.

So five months of hard graft had come to an end as the countdown to July 25th 2008 had begun, Trowbridge snooker club being the venue – not quite Vegas, but you can't have it all. Just thinking of the date gave me nervous butterflies, but there was an overwhelming sense of excitement to go with it – I couldn't wait. The one thing I believed I would have over my opponent come fight night was experience, which counts for a lot in this game. Sure, the fear factor would be there in me, but my years of amateur experience going to smoke-filled social clubs or sport centres up and down the country meant that I would be more comfortable with the atmosphere and feel more relaxed, especially if I had some U2 and Elvis belting my eardrums before fighting time was called.

Any slight advantage over your opponent should be gratefully accepted. Let's get it on! After 22 years of contemplating and five months of a ball-breaking training regime I'd committed myself to, my personal night of destiny had arrived. I was sat on the train for the very last time with my music playing, feeling very relaxed, confident and going over my fight plan again and again. Details of my opponent were revealed to me at my last gym session as we was having a warm down. It became apparent to me he wasn't well liked around the Trowbridge area – something of a bully was a common description, and knocking his lights out was the common request. As simple as it may seem from outside the ropes, actually doing it is another thing, so I was picking away at Mark as to what he knew of him and what I was to expect. He told me he was a young lad from the town who had a lot of junior amateur bouts but then stopped, became the town bully. He was still working on his fitness, but was a tough fucker with a big punch that would knock me out if caught clean enough. Having a couple of days to think it over I came to the game plan of boxing him from a distance, creating openings. Then when the opportunity was there to step in with my own combinations I wouldn't give him time to settle himself and to let go with his own power shots. I could sense that being the home boy with his family, friends and girlfriend being there he'd want to take me out of there quickly as possible, so I predicted him swinging his thumping right hand, trying to dislodge my pretty chin from my face and falling right into my fight plan.

Arriving at the venue munching a banana I was given directions to where all the boxers changed and as I entered what was a large bar area with tables and chairs, I was greeted by my fellow gym mates and gladiators on the same bill. After firm handshakes and man hugs all round we checked out the ring and its surroundings. As we were chatting, in walked my opponent with that chav look about him, and an 'I'm the geezer' swagger. We had a distant eye-to-eye and I returned back to my mates. My next appointment was with the doctor for the routine medical check and weigh-in; I passed with healthy honours and weighed a lean 13 stones. Oh those days of fighting at 10 stone seemed a long way away!

Back upstairs and the atmosphere where we were changing was very passive and relaxed, not a sight of guys chomping at the bit or bashing holes in walls – in fact it was very much the opposite with some laughter and friendly banter being exchanged between one another. The overwhelming thing that hit you when you walked into the room was the bloody heat — it was unbelievably hot up there. I don't think air conditioning had made it to Trowbridge just yet. I was fifth fight on the menu, so I wanted to be in my boots and shorts wearing a sleeveless T-shirt warming up long before I was due to go on. So I found myself a quiet corner and went about my business. After my prep time I decided to go downstairs and sample the atmosphere while watching the first few bouts. As I danced on my nimble toes staying relaxed, I could see him chatting with his group of supporters. One-by-one heads were turning in my direction as he pointed me out to them. You could say that it was a bit of gamesmanship, but I figured that if they got to see who their boy was fighting, and to see the confident cockiness I was showing, they would encourage him to knock me out thus providing me with the opportunities to box and move and execute my plan to the book.

So far things were going to plan and I couldn't wait to get in there. The time wasn't so far away, so back upstairs to the inferno. I went more to get myself into a good mental state of mind. Over and over again I repeated to myself, 'Can't be beat, won't be beat, can't be beat, won't be beat', telling myself that over the five months I've been training my arse off, no one was going to beat me tonight – especially not that young punk across the way. I've trained too hard for this and I'm not letting my travelling support of 36 friends and girlfriend Trudy down – more importantly I wasn't going to let myself down. This was my opportunity to go out on that win I always fought for in my amateur days. Trudy had been with me from the beginning, encouraging me along the way even though secretly I knew she thought I was mad to be doing it, along with my mum who I'm sure she'd had many a discussion with about the taboo subject.

I was warming up on the pads when the call for fight time is called. I pause at the top of the stairs waiting for the 'King' to announce my imminent arrival to the gladiators – Coliseum? Well, not quite, but you can use your imagination. The King called me – 'Bright lights city gonna set my soul, gonna set my soul on fire' – that was my cue. As I walked across the landing and down the stairs the atmosphere was amazing. My friends and neutrals were doing a great stomping rendition of 'Viva Las Vegas' that would befit a world champion the likes of Nigel Benn or Frank Bruno, it was belting! I deliberately stood at the foot of the steps of the ring just to hear another chorus. I was so relaxed by the time I ducked under the ropes to a rapturous applause from my lot in the far corner. His entrance went unnoticed as he came in to some rap music shite. No going back now, as the ref called us both to the centre of the ring for his instructions and the familiar eye-to-eye glare. One of the first things you're taught when starting out in boxing is that the eyes tell you everything you need to know. They show fear, nervousness, anger, and as I looked into his they showed me all I needed to know.

We came to the centre of the ring for round one and I started with my rod-like jab, whilst keeping an eye on that cocked right hand of his. It was great to be back. As predicted he swung the right hand in my direction. I stepped back away from it and stepped straight back in with my own landing flush on his designer stubble chin. As my old fella use to say to me, 'Always get the first punch in me son,' which is what I did, and boy did he feel it. To his credit he took it well and came back with some of his own. The first round went like a dream: he was blowing hard, trying to connect with the big shots while I was moving around bobbing and weaving, then counter-punching with my own shots. The round ended with a touch of gloves and a wink as we went back to our corners for a small beverage and chit-chat from our seconds.

The second round started and I wanted to step it up a bit and work him hard so I dug in a couple of body shots to begin with then thought to myself, 'I wonder if I can try this with him?' I jabbed a couple of lefts to his body then fainted with one and came upstairs to land a big right hand right on the button followed by a three-punch combination, each one landing hard and bringing a moan of pain from him. I thought at this point he was on his way down, but he stood up well to grab on to me until his head cleared. I went on to win the round convincingly with more neat boxing and moving. The round finished with another touch of gloves – we've both earned one another's respect by this stage.

The third and final round started with both sets of supporters shouting encouragement, mine wanting me to win the round safely and his wanting to see me flat on my back counting light bulbs. As in the two previous rounds my boxing took over. No matter how hard he tried, he fell for the jab to the body followed by the booming right again and I just saw his punches coming every time. Fair play to him, he took my solid shots on the chin and stayed upright, although I'm sure he wanted to go down by this time but didn't want to in front of his home crowd. The last 20 seconds or so of the fight I danced and moved knowing that the result was a cert. As for his big right hand knocking me out, well I think I took three clear shots on the chin and it weren't all it was cracked up to be. At the final bell we both hugged each other and said, 'Well done' then I went over to my side where my supporters were to pump my fist in the air in celebration of the pending result. They all looked like they were enjoying the result as much as I was about to. The announcement was made proper a few minutes later and at that moment the months of hard work and the twenty-two years of disappointment were all behind me and forgotten about, and to this day it remains my personal favourite achievement. On the funny side of it though, I always remember the cries of 'boo' coming from his section of supporters as I was enjoying my moment. I felt like the pantomime villain who's just beaten their local lad – actually, I guess I was... he he he!

It was a great feeling to go over to my mates still sweating and carrying blotches of his blood on my arms and shoulders. Bless them all, it didn't stop them wanting to give me a huge hug and the girls giving me a kiss on the cheek, but the best hug and kiss was from a tearful Trudy who had gone through this journey with me and had to sit through it all as some local nutter wanted to take my head off with everything he had. Love ya babe.

Everyone was very complimentary of my performance and the shouts for 'drink' were deafening. Upstairs in the changing room where it was still bloody hot, the lads were very happy with the result and were more than happy to see him take a beating, but besides all of that it was pleasing to win again – something that the judges had denied me in the amateurs. I knew how good I was, even if they didn't like my style or whatever it was. I'm very pleased to have done this to prove to myself that I wasn't the loser my record suggested I was. I doubt Frank Warren or Don King will be on the phone offering me that title shot but hey, who cares? As every fighter wants, whether they are a champion, journeyman or a trier like me, when they retire they want to end it on their terms and with a win. I did and I'm more than happy to leave it at that. These days I'm a fully qualified coach of Bath City Boxing Club and I love being there doing what Maxi started, Sid and Marion nurtured and Mark finished.

Nineteen
More But Brief

I've had a lot of good times travelling and I hope some of my memories inspire you and other people to do likewise. I've got a lot of stories to tell but those I've written about rank as some of my favourites. But here are some more stories and places in brief....

Bombay
For some reason I've met people who think this place is beautiful. I first went there with the *Song of Flower* and I was so disgusted with the place I couldn't wait to get out of it. And I'd hoped I never go there again. Wrong!

As part of the world cruise on board the *Crystal Symphony* I was to go Bombay again. I'm sorry but the place is a shit-hole and it stinks! You can literally see human sewage flowing down the streets to the blocked drains at the end of them. Which, I might add, was usually where the street dogs would hang out.

Another thing that shocked me were the 'cages'. Our taxi driver took us through the red light area of the city and out of the window you could see these doorways covered up by a curtain and then a cell-like door closed in front of them. They had about 15 of them in a row. I asked the driver if it was true, what we'd just seen.

In his true Indian accent he replied, 'Yes sir, those are the prostitutes and those little rooms are their places of business.'

All that is in them is a bed inside a room no bigger than prison cell, with just the curtain as privacy, hence the word 'cages'. I'm no prude about these things but that just disgusted me, and to think that they like to blame Africa or gay people for the Aids virus. People should come down to the 'cages' and see what goes on there.

Nah, I'm sorry guys I don't agree with ya on that one!

Saigon was more respectable than those animals, and more beautiful than that dump of a city.

San Francisco

The one other big thing that San Francisco has going for it besides being a beautiful city is the sail-in. It was another early morning arrival surrounded by a crisp beautiful breeze that greeted us as we slowly approached the Golden Gate Bridge. To be perfectly honest with you, although I was impressed by the bridge, I was a little disappointed at its actual size. It wasn't as big as I thought it would be and I'm quite sure that I've seen bigger here in England. But nevertheless, the fact that it's probably the most famous and well known bridge in the world makes it all the more special to be sailing underneath it.

You can understand why it's called the Golden Gate because as the sun hits its impressive structure it gives off a golden red glow – it is quite spectacular.

Once you've cleared the bridge up in the distance to your left you can see... Alcatraz. And what a spooky, eerie looking place it looks as well, with its deserted buildings and exercise yards. It looks a very daunting and intimidating place. To have been on its long distinguished guest list would 'ave sent a few frightening shivers down anyone's back as the judge passed sentence. Al Capone and 'Baby Face' Nelson being only but a few of them – oh, and Clint Eastwood, or was that just a movie?

It's been open to the public for tours for some time now and it was something I wanted to do but on this occasion I couldn't pay anyone to work for me. Instead I managed a few beers in a club with friends during the overnight stay – maybe next time.

Monte Carlo

I've talked about places like Cannes and Rio having money, but Monte Carlo is not short of a few francs either.

I've been lucky enough to have been there quite a few times now and I still find it a beautiful and thrilling place to be in. The way the port is a circular shape and the buildings are built, it looks like they've been placed on top of one another – it's very similar to Hong Kong harbour actually.

It's always been my ambition to see a Formula 1 race there. It must be the best place to see one of those races as the drivers weave around through the tight street circuit. The closest I've come is two days before and two days after the race, just as the stands are being put up or just as they are taken down. One day I will.

It's a great place to enjoy yourself as you can imagine. I've been pissed there many a time. On the far side of the harbour is a place called Stars & Bars. It's an American-style bar with an upstairs club that was once taken over by the rock star Prince who played an impromptu gig one night, just before the ship arrived. Gutted!

When I get my yacht it's the first place I'm sailing to. I think I'd enjoy lazing around in the sun sipping champagne and beers amongst the other beautiful boats tied up.

Oh... and don't forget the G-string girlfriends.

Rhode Island

Remember the family who were on board during our visit to St Petersburg and how myself and other members of the bar and casino department looked after their teenage son and daughter?

Well, Rhode Island was their hometown port and as promised they sent their son Danny, who looked real pleased to see us again, to pick us up in a hired mini-bus. I think there were about 12 or 13 of us, all ready to spend some time at their home.

After about ten minutes of listening to some extremely loud rock music we finally arrived at the beautiful grand-looking house that was almost lost amongst the surrounding trees at the end of a pebble driveway. Danny made sure he was out of the van before anyone and was up the steps of the house knocking on the door. As the door opened it revealed the whole family standing there with glasses of champagne! We were all speechless. We never anticipated this. After the firm hugs, handshakes and welcomes we were lead into the large lounge area that was surrounded with glass sliding doors showing us the beauty of the garden and stream below.

It was a beautiful house with old wooden beams overhead with an old stone fireplace standing proud of its surroundings. Under our feet was a beautifully polished timber floor with a grand piano in the corner looking like it had just come out of its box.

As we walked further into the room we could see that they'd prepared a huge salad bar with everything you could think of, as well as three chafing dishes with hot curry, chilli and bolognaise inside. Once again we were speechless but we gave a big round of well-deserved applause. To think that someone appreciated the service we gave on board and to return the gesture by doing this was far, far more pleasing then receiving a cash tip.

We were there a good few hours during which time we drunk more champagne, wine and beers and finished of the food. Then we took a walk around the grounds they owned. What's really sad though is that I can only remember the son's name – the rest of the family is a blank. But I'll never forget their generosity and the genuine appreciation from the whole family. It was a very special day had by all so I'm gonna call them 'The Cool Family'.

Acapulco

When I read the ships itinerary (MS *Silvercloud*) I was happy to discover that we'd be having an overnight stay down Acapulco way. Amongst my ambitions already written about, another one of them was to watch the cliff divers of La Quebrada.

So upon arrival myself and my Scottish cabin mate Robert headed for the taxi-ranks outside. The divers perform twice a day, at one o'clock and then eleven o'clock in the evening. We managed to see the afternoon show, which was as daring as I imagined it to be.

You first enter the cove and immediately you focus on the height of the cliffs to the shallow waters below. As the time gets closer the crowds are gathering to the viewing terrace that overlooks the whole area, as well as the terrace restaurant that looks like it's clinging to the cliff's edge.

Then a small fleet of fishing boats turn up, each carrying up to two or three divers. The swells of the ocean lift the boats up and down as the divers attempt to take the applause of the waiting crowds. Then it's into the water. As if the dive is not dangerous enough, these guys let the swells take them to the foot of the cliffs from where they try to anticipate the best moment to climb out of the water. If they get it wrong they could quite easily be cut and battered against the jagged rocks. Then they've got the steep climb to the first diving position. They each dive from, dare I say, the lowest level (which still looks bloody fearsome to me) just to get the crowd going, and I guess it helps to settle their nerves as well. These guys are no taller than five feet but they've got a huge heart and balls of brass and nerves of steel.

Each one gives the cross sign across his chest, then patiently waits for the ocean swell to come in and fill the cove with deep water. You have to really see it to appreciate the guts of these guys y'know – one slight mistake and the guy could be killed on the rocks under the shallow waters. As the show progresses the divers go even higher and higher, but now they're including twists and turns on the way down. Each dive is warmly applauded by an enthusiastic crowd that has grown to about 300 people.

By now the divers are feeling confident and are now going down in pairs, giving it a spectacular look as they enter the water together. The Grand Finale is the highest peak. This must be high because it takes the diver a few minutes to say a prayer to the Holy Mary statue and to compose himself while he waits for the perfect moment to go over.

Being amongst the crowd you can feel the collective nervous atmosphere. We aren't the ones up there but you can feel your heart beating like crazy. Then, as if in slow motion, he leaps out and away from the cliff edge and into his swan dive to catch the warm waters below.

And the crowd go wild! It really is breath-taking and is money well spent as the guys come round looking for donations for their heroics.

The other thing I wanted to do whilst here in sunny Acapulco was to paraglide above Acapulco bay, so I did. And while I was up there I did a dance with my legs hanging while I sang the words high above the shark infested waters – 'Going loco down in Acapulco'. If me mates could see me now!

Now I did say this was an overnight stay, so come the evening we were off into town. We ended up at an amazing nightclub called 'Extravaganza'. It's perched high on one of the hills that overlook the whole bay and the whole of two sides of it is made of glass, with the glass dance floor looking like it is suspended in thin air. I mean these glass walls were about 70 feet tall and along the window it had a catwalk which you could dance upon. The big kick was that if you turned to face the evening outside you felt like you were dancing high in the air above Acapulco Bay. It was one big trip. Then at around midnight from the roof of the club you have a fireworks eruption going off, which lights up the whole bay. It looked like someone had started a war from the rooftops.

That is definitely one place I would recommend seeing on your travels.

London

London for me is too close to home and it's not one of my favourite places either. I have a kind of love-hate relationship with the place y'know, I enjoy visiting it, but then I can't wait to get the hell out of it. I often wonder if anyone else feels the same as me.

But I must admit that I got a real pleasure at actually sailing up, and down, the Thames.

Starting at the mouth with Canvey Island on your starboard side (the right), you first start seeing the sights about three miles out of town. Along the way what's really nice about it is that you pass all the posh apartments on the river bank and almost everyone flashes their house lights on and off as a mark of saying 'hello', as well as the ones from out on the balconies.

And of course you sail past a building site, which is always funny because the builders always drop their pants to 'moony' us. We the crew members, being away from the passengers at the back of the ship, always returned the gesture to them, applauded warmly from both parties. From the river you get a whole different view of London – it's really good. But getting closer to Tower Bridge is the highlight for me. You can see the roadblocks coming down to stop the traffic and either side of the bridge is packed with people ready to wave as you pass underneath. The drivers of the cars are out leaning over the wall as if to say, 'Well I might as well see what the fuss is about.'

As the captain sounds the ship's horn, everyone either side of the bridge, along the footpaths and along the riverbank wave like mad. The experience gets really grand as the draw-bridge raises and the ship sails majestically under as the crowds continue to wave, shout and whistle furiously. As you continue to sail through, the journey ends at the *HMS Belfast* as the ship is tied up alongside – and the rest of London can go about its business.

To think that you stopped the whole of London for 20 minutes or so really did give me a buzz!

Portofino

This small secluded port belonging to the Italian Riviera is an absolutely beautiful tranquil place to see. Unbeknown to me at the time, it was a rich men's playground for the famous. I just thought it was your typical council estate for the well-to-do, but apparently it's got a few well known and rich neighbours.

The old original buildings still painted in yellows, greens, reds and blues surround the horseshoe shape harbour with the local fishing boats tied up. It has a cosmopolitan square filled with the elegant restaurants and cappuccino houses around the outside, leaving the old cobbled stone surface open for the bandstands or as catwalks for the fashion conscious dames – bloody murder in those high heels though, I bet. But what's really nice about it is the fact that it combines the old traditional fishing port, with its old men and women still hand-making the fishing nets, with its high-class clientele. To me it's a very unique place – there's not very many of them left that the average tourist trade hasn't destroyed. Mind you, I think the price of the cappuccinos might have something to do with that.

I used to always look forward to seeing Portofino listed on the ship's itinerary. For me it was pure relaxation time while having a caffeine fix of the best quality with the local tiramisu. No traffic, no annoying scooters whizzing past you and not one English football shirt in sight. If you take a trip up through the old cobbled streets you arrive at the old church on top of the hill that overlooks the whole harbour – from there you get the most picturesque view you could wish for. One trip to that place and you were ready for what the evening had in store for you on board ship.

Los Angeles – Revisited
'Only in America,' as Don King says.

It was in November of '99 that my wife Casey and I were in the States visiting family. During one of the many days just sitting back enjoying the time away from freezing cold England, I was sat watching the news channel as a story was developing on live TV.

During prime time television a man was on the run in a high-speed chase along the freeway with three cop cars in pursuit. As the story was unfolding, more and more other news stations were getting in on the act until it was being shown on every news channel there was. I was getting more and more intrigued by this, because by now there were around ten cop cars, two police helicopters and about five news helicopters, all in pursuit. It was discovered that the driver had failed to pull over when asked to because he had pending car fines to be paid – car fines! When making a run for it the police officers believed there was a gun inside the vehicle, so therefore decided the man was armed and dangerous.

The cops studied a map and anticipated that with a full tank of fuel the man was heading for the Mexican border, so they had roadblocks set up in preparation. This was getting exciting I tell ya – you almost felt like you wanted the guy to have a full tank just to prolong his pursuit.

Bono describes the America he sees in a U2 song by saying, 'You can't tell the difference between ABC news and Hillstreet Blues.' Well, at this moment it was true because you couldn't see a difference between fact and fiction, because although it was real life it was getting as exciting as watching an episode of Hillstreet Blues.

Anyway, as the bad guy was weaving in between traffic the whole afternoon had passed. The cops figured that he'd be running low pretty soon, a few miles short of his freedom over the border, so without causing any danger they sat patiently behind him - during which time the man could be seen waving something in the air from his side window that looked like a gun.

As the evening sun was setting the car started to noticeably slow down - the car was now running on fumes and the LAPD were starting to swarm around him from the front, sides and back until he came to a halt. This was the moment the whole audience, in a sick way, were waiting for. As they all came to a stop the car doors opened and each cop inside took cover behind with their pistols taking aim. The coverage for us the audience was coming directly above from one of the many news helicopters, so we could see everything real close up.

The chief of police instructed the driver to get out of the car and step away with his hands in the air. As he did this the driver made the action of reaching for a gun concealed under his T-shirt - big mistake right there! Without any hesitation every cop opened fire on the guy, sending puffs of deep red mist into the early evening air as his body crashed to the asphalt. I could just hear in my head some news director shouting at his cameraman,

'Keep rolling, keep rolling guys this is great news.' And to make sure the guy was dead they even sent over an Alsatian dog to rip at his body parts. I guess it was standard for that to happen, but I'm pretty sure the guy was dead after being filled with a ton of lead.

I was speechless - this was live TV. By the time we got to look at this on the news again later, it'd been edited down not to show the bloody ending, but it was quite shocking to actually see someone blown away like that for real.

This happened over two years ago (at the time of writing) and I can still remember it quite clearly. The whole drama was headline news that evening, all because it was caught on live news cameras. Living in England this type of thing is never seen on the telly, so I was pretty quiet afterwards, but the in-laws just sat there and shrugged their shoulders as if to say, 'Hey we see it all the time it's nothing new.' They then proceeded to compare stories of past car chases they'd seen on live TV with 'bloodier' endings.

Don King has a point!

Twenty

The Crew Bar

During everyone's first day on board ship, after the formalities of signing forms and handing over your passport to the crew steward, the first question people ask their fellow crew members is, 'Where is and how good is the crew bar?' Not a hint of 'How hard is the work or how is my new boss, how many hours is he or she going to work me?' Noooo!

It's the location of the heart and soul of any ship, regarded by crew as the place where, for the next six months, it's all going to happen for them - a place where they can escape from the bullshit going on upstairs, where cigar-smoking attitudes constantly grapple with the next person about how much money they have or how many times that they've sailed with the company before, and how each year the captain of the ship sends them Christmas cards. And that pathetic gesture that is supposed to make you feel warm and welcome - yes that's right, the old kissing on the cheeks from about two inches away from their plastic faces, followed by the 'Mmma, Mmma'. What's that all about eh? I think you can kinda understand where I'm coming from here yeah.

So anyway....

The place where we could be ourselves because at the end of the day the uniform comes off, no matter what position you are upstairs - in the same way the uniform might come off from the simplest of jobs. Forget about the stripes when you're shooting a tequila slammer with the staff captain or the hotel director, just don't go shouting your mouth off about anything that is meant to be secret within work yeah, 'cos the next morning it's work as usual! 'Loose lips sink ships', as the saying goes.

For me personally, having fun and a social life is just as important as taking your job seriously upstairs, so it's an important place for me. After a long day running around pleasing six star guests I was never one for going straight to bed, as a lot of people

I've met over the years will probably tell you, so finding the right social scene was very important. What you have to understand, you people who have never worked on board a ship before, is that this is our home for six months and we have to eat, drink and live with people who we've never met before for the whole of that period. It's a unique lifestyle let me tell you – sometimes you get along and sometimes you don't. Which makes your close friends all the more important and needed – after all it gets boring after a while, going ashore alone or drinking by yourself.

I've been fortunate to have had some great times and met some really good, genuine, nice people that I still keep in touch with today via the beauty of the internet. It all stems from a good social life on board, created by a good crew steward and lots of hard working Filipinos – a lot of activities wouldn't happen if not for them setting things up and working the bars. Cheers guys!

The great thing about our crew bar, which makes me chuckle every time, is that it's always been the centre of gossip and intrigue for the paying passengers upstairs. These people have paid thousands to come on board to sample or live the life that they have come accustomed to, and all they want to do is to find out who is shagging who and whereabouts the crew bar is located, and whether they can come down to it? As if they're not happy with life upstairs they want to interfere with ours downstairs as well. Bog off!

The bar itself will be doubled up as a recreation room during the day or a getaway for the smokers. At night it will come alive with a mini nightclub feel to it and the cheesiest neon lights hanging from the walls or ceilings, with someone providing the music from his or her CD collection. Depending on the DJ's nationality we will be listening to an array of music from heavy metal to dance from reggae to rock – not everyone's cuppa tea some nights, but you're so busy chatting and drinking that you don't really care.

What's really funny about this place is that it's regarded by female folk as a 'meat market' with them being classed as the meat, but we all have to have some companionship and fun don't we? Yeah, okay, I can agree with them to some extent, but we were all still young and available, and out for a good time as well as anyone else, male or female. And believe me that stuff goes on with everybody, stripes or no stripes, and could be another book altogether.

On other occasions we sometimes found solitude just sitting amongst friends in their cabin, with late night chats, Chardonnay and a small feast from room service... unofficially.

And depending on your tropical location or the weather outside it was always nice to sit out on the outside crew deck just watching the stars and feeling the warm sea air – I remember those nights with great fondness. I've always said that the best skies at night are at sea and I will remain saying so till I die. The stillness of the ocean with the reflections of the moon following us everywhere we sailed, shooting stars catching our attention – it genuinely brings me to tears every time I think back to those nights.

I also remember the nights which took a lot of explaining the morning after, but that comes later.

Towards the end of the month the crew steward would arrange a deck party, complete with bar, decorations and a DJ, and on some occasions live music with help from crew welfare funds. The head chef would arrange the food and anyone not on duty would be expected to give a helping hand with the set-up – a great team effort on everyone's part. Each party always had a theme to it, giving the opportunity for everyone to expand their imagination in coming up with some fancy dress outfits. Over the years I've seen Caribbean parties, pirates and convicts, hospital, uniform changes, samba – you name it, and some of the costumes that these people have come up with have been outrageous, hilarious and some risqué ones too.

The one thing that really surprises me, even today, is the energy that we summoned up for these occasions – it's the old saying, 'work hard play hard', taking over. Understand it like this. The normal people living at home ashore mostly work Monday to Friday, for an average of 40 to 50 hours a week, then have their social life on a weekend. We work seven days a week for six months with no days off, each week consisting of 70-plus hours, and during that time we are expected to have ourselves a social life. So where do we get the energy from I ask myself? Personally I think it comes from the adrenalin rush we get when the ship's whistle goes off telling us its the end of our shift — it doesn't really do that, but you get the same rush. During the day you've chatted with your mates about joining them for a beer or two later, or whether they will be attending the crew party, then when you're set free you go for it and then suffer the consequences the following morning... the hangover! And there's nothing worse than a hangover at sea! But then it's all worth it when you talk and laugh about it the following morning in the crew mess and see the photographs a couple of days later.

And amazingly enough you're doing exactly the same the following night not long after the hangover died off. But it's the enjoyment of socializing with the different nationalities, something that you wouldn't be doing on a normal weekend back home, that gives you that buzz to do it all over again. And speaking from a guy's point of view, it's the possibility of getting to know one of the many girls on board. You never know you might even take home a girlfriend with you after your contract has finished, or at least the experience of having done your bit for world relations. I'd like to think I've done my bit for Queen and Country! Ha, Ha, Ha!

I remember during a contract on board the *Crystal Symphony* I took the party occasion a little too far and paid the price for it... but it was worth it though.

It all started one day when we were in Mexico somewhere and my cabin mate Leslie, an English guy who was also my best mate, was celebrating his birthday. He paid the other bartenders to work his shifts so that he could go out all day to have some beers and tequila, as you do when it's your 40th.

During the day all the other bar staff joined him for a drink after their shift had finished, then left when they had to restart. It's safe to say that he wasn't celebrating alone and wasn't the only one that staggered back to the ship slightly intoxicated!

Upon his return later that night the party continued in the crew bar, where everyone was jam-packed inside and dancing to the loud beats of the music while drinking the lime-wedged Corona bottles and tequila body shots (providing you found a willing participant).

Everyone was swinging the night away, including Les surprisingly enough, but it wasn't long before his alcoholic endeavours caught up with him, so being an old man we carried him off to bed, made sure he was comfortable, and then returned to the Mexican soirée that was continuing. Hours later the party finished to everyone's disappointment, but that only encouraged us to start parties elsewhere. Everyone had their own venues and guest lists, including me, so it was back to my place. We found Leslie happily sleeping off his 40th year with a growing hangover we could physically watch maturing!

So the music was on and the drinks were flowing once more, with not a murmur from Les. It was then that a voice in my ear took over and a devil appeared on my shoulder:

'Just look at those eyebrows, aren't those the best eyebrows you've ever seen, don't you just wanna shave them off?!'

Just then the pretty little angel appeared on my other shoulder pleading with me:

'No Sean don't do it, he's your best mate he'll be ever so upset with you.'

Before I knew it an argument had developed between the good and bad side of my conscience – what was I to do?!

The answer: 'Shave 'em off!'

As I'd come to this decision we were four in the room: another English guy called Mike, Beatrix and Shonda, one of whom had recently bought a new camcorder and so ran off to fetch it while I was preparing the shaving cream.

With the director in position and calling for 'action' I proceeded slowly (and very professionally I might add) to 'whip 'em off', while the other two had started to paint his fingers and toe nails pink with nail varnish!

To this day I don't know how I managed to keep a steady hand without causing injury, because the tears of laughter were flowing down my cheeks, along with everyone else taking part! I'm still laughing to myself as I'm writing this for you now.

After about 20 minutes the job was completed and what a sight Leslie was, lying there with one eyebrow missing and his fingers and toes... pink! We screamed so loud I thought I was going to stop breathing or shit myself, and not once did Leslie move throughout the whole time, it was incredible!

As the night came to an end we all departed to catch some sleep, still with the thought of Leslie's new looks in our minds.

The following morning I was shaken out of bed to the enormous screams coming from the bathroom:

'What the f**k!!'

All kinds of scenarios ran through my head during those split seconds until I realised that Leslie had risen first only to discover his new fashion statement.

'You bastard!' he shouted. The abuse that came out of that little shower room was unrepeatable. In my confusion I'd forgotten about the activities of the previous night until he made his entrance back in to the room to confront me. Well, let me tell ya, to this day I have never seen anything as funny or rib-cracking in my life. The tears of laughter re-appeared and I felt for sure that I was definitely going to die this time – I didn't know laughing could be so painful!

'Ah mate, how could you do this to me,' was his plea. I didn't have a sensible reply so I didn't bother trying 'cos I hadn't stopped laughing yet.

He went back into the bathroom to assess the situation a bit more and came to the conclusion that he couldn't go to work with one eyebrow missing, so it was in his best interests to 'whip' off the other one. This didn't really help my cause as I was rolling around the cabin floor knocking on laughter's door! And it certainly didn't ease the tension as he went storming off to work shouting, 'I'm gonna tell the captain about this,' with the ordeal of having to face guests and fellow crew members staring at him, still to come.

Within minutes of him leaving the anticipated phone call arrived, and I, along with everyone else involved, was called the bar manager's office, prompt! And for the record, I was quite prepared to face the firing squad alone but the other guys volunteered to give themselves up.

After the ear-bashing from our boss we were taken to a captain's meeting in his quarters, where every head of department and senior officers were present. A trial at sea if you like! So there we were, the four of us, outside the captain's suite ready to face a possible sacking, still bloody laughing!

The door opens, 'Jenkins,' a loud voice shouts. I enter the room still wiping tears from my cheeks to see all the top-dogs in a crescent-shape seating arrangement, with the captain in the middle. It may only be a cruise ship but you still have to present yourself like a naval officer would.

'Sean Jenkins, crew number 505, Bar Department, Sir.'

He just looked at me all blank.

As he then proceeded to read out the charges brought against me I could do nothing but replay the whole event in my head, and I couldn't help but want to break into fits of laughter again. So I did what was necessary to save what job prospects I still had left, which was to firmly set my eyes on the carpet and think of what sandwiches a Russian tractor driver might be eating right now on his lunch break in a freezing cold field in St Petersburg! Anything but Leslie's eyebrows.

I almost lost it at one stage during the hearing, as I gazed up at the jury in front of me – I could see them looking down at the carpet sniggering away, probably thinking of the same Russian tractor driver and his sandwich selection!

The end came as a big relief to me as I admitted the offense and was instructed to sign my first and final written warning, then told to leave and send in the next culprit. I've kept the warning and placed it in my treasured albums, and it always makes for a good laugh when anybody comes across it and wants to know the story. As for the video of the events, well you'll just have to search the comedy section of your local Blockbuster.

A few years ago I tried making contact with Leslie but he never returned my calls - understandable I guess, but if you're reading this Les, sorry mate it was only a bit of fun.

The things I did in my wild young teen years eh!

I'd also like to mention that over the years I've really enjoyed the nights listening to somebody, usually a Filipino, strumming on an acoustic guitar belting out any song at request: the usual *Unchained Melody* or *American Pie* were always everyone's favourites. I'm sure past and present crew members reading this can appreciate what I'm saying here, — we've all had those nights.

My philosophy with life on board was always the same: a happy ship downstairs is a happy ship upstairs. And I'd like to think that my motto was being carried out by crew members on all ships at sea today.

If only the rest of the world could get on with each other as we did on board our happy ship.

Twenty-One
The Tourists Have Landed

The art of spotting a tourist from miles away has become easier and easier due to the years of looking after them on board the ships or hotels I've worked over the years. It can become an amusing way to spend the afternoon in some coffee shop here or abroad, just tourist/people watching – everybody does it. Pay extra attention for the Americans, they're the easiest. I know they bring large amounts of revenue everywhere they go, and this is by no way meant as a cheap shot at them, but a rather side-tickling way of helping you spot them while you wait for your 'froffy' coffee.

The White Trainers
What is it with our American friends and their fascination with white trainers? Of all the wide range of colours available to us in this day and age of fashion, why do they persist with only white?! I can understand the comfort of a decent pair of trainers with all the walking involved visiting a new country, but why white? They make you stand out like a turkey at Christmas time. Go and speak with your fashion consultants for some better advice, even better have them fired and let your grandchildren dress you! You've been made a mockery of for years, now it's time to get even.

This brings me to my second observation....

The Colombo-Style Rain Mac
Whenever it's raining, which is quite often here in England, 'What's with the mac... Jack?!'

You obviously don't know, but here in England we regard that as a 'dirty old man's' jacket.

So anyone seen wearing it is seen as a very dodgy character indeed. And it's taken some serious stick over the years from a nation that is known for its dry sense of humour, so don't be surprised if you get some funny looks from some smirking local resident. Another sackable offense for your fashion adviser.

Next....

The Baseball Cap

I always thought the red and white Marlboro caps were all dead and buried by now, but no! Not according to our friends across the pond. Granted they are worn by the older generation of Americans, but you would have thought that some hip and trendy member of the family would have bought a more fashionable style of cap for his old man or granddad. Some thing like 'NY Giants', 'LA Lakers', 'Go USA' or even 'Homer Rules', something that would make him a hip-looking older guy still clinging to his youth, get what I mean. Come on guys, don't you want your father to look 'cool'?

The Video-Camcorder

It still baffles me even today that when I see a tourist in town, or leaving the gangway to search out the pleasures of the exciting new port they find themselves in, why oh why do they have the most expensive camcorder hanging so casually over their shoulders? It's as if they leave their own countries without their common sense, leaving themselves wide open to the leeches that prey on their naive way of thinking.

I can always remember the day I passed an older couple as they stepped off a gangway. The gentlemen was carrying a camera over one shoulder and a camcorder over the other, with his eye constantly in the view-finder, not even watching where he was going, and his wife carrying a bag that was wide open, looking for directions from a map. Come on guys, be sensible would ya? I know I'm having a bit of fun with you right now, but that's not to say I wouldn't want you going home without everything you came with, including your health. Just because you don't see anyone looking suspicious hanging around the port gates it doesn't mean they haven't 'clocked' you.

The Coffee-Shop/Restaurant

Having worked in coffee shops and restaurants myself, after a real busy day running around like a mad-man there's nothing worse or more irritating than having someone come in as you're starting to wind down. So I would find it really amusing watching the last remaining travellers come in and sit there for about ten minutes studying the menu before realising that they order what they want at the bar or counter, depending on the establishment. After they work it out they still come to you: 'Do we order with you sir?' says the very polite Yank. 'Sorry we're closing now,' I'd reply, with a sympathetic face.

It was always a way of gaining revenge for the most difficult ones that you had earlier in the day and you were looking for someone to take it out on. Staff within the catering trade always have a way of having the last laugh.

Anyway, I hope I've not upset anyone by my amusing observations during the endless hours sat in coffee shops and bars all over the would just people watching. If I have, then tough!

Twenty-Two
New Orleans

There's something about the great Mississippi that can be mentioned in the same conversation as the Nile of Cairo, the Thames of London, or the Amazon of South America, in that they can stand tall with a clenched fist, as if to say 'Come on guys, lets hang out together.' I think it's the sheer strength and the powerful images that they portray when people think of the countries that they dissect. The river in question is quite an impressive flow of water with its undercurrents and its wide stretches gripping the surrounding banks – you can almost hear its roar.

My first knowledge of the famous river was in the books of Tom Sawyer and Huckleberry Finn that I read when I was a kid at school, and the river boats were their means of travel. Some of you might be saying it was the Missouri not the Mississippi that they used to hang around, but it's only a name isn't it? Anyway, I've grown up to associate it with the Mississippi, with the two young fellas, so there and the mud-pie as well.

I was on board the *Silver Whisper* on this occasion travelling to the great city of New Orleans and was a recent new arrival to the ship, so a lot of the people and faces were still new to me. I think I was only there about five days and had been working late in the bar, so everyone had gone ahead of me with the promise to keep a look out for me. Bourbon Street was the destination, so it's not to difficult to find a rowdy bunch of crew members amongst its décor. Sure enough I found them but they were heading off in the opposite direction... home! They'd gone off at a startling pace, without thinking of pacing themselves, so come 1.30 am they were shot. So off they went in one direction and I in the other. I'm an independent sort of guy, so drinking alone was not to bother me 'cos New Orleans being the place it is, you quickly find a friend or make conversation with someone.

My drinking buddy for this occasion was Edmund. He was an old black guy who was homeless, polite and looked like he had the whole of his life written across his face – a black version of Keith Richards if you like. Let me explain.

I had come to a point in the night when I needed to hear some blues and jazz music, so I started to walk down Bourbon Street on the search for such a place. I decided to stop this old black man standing on a corner under a street lamp for some advice/directions. As I approached him I could hear his pleas to the passing party people falling short so I offered him a business proposition: 'Show me a decent blues/jazz bar around here and I'll pay for your night in the local YMCA and enough for breakfast as well.' He snapped my hand as if it was going to be his last meal.

As we started to walk I made it quite clear to him I was no tourist and not to take me for a ride or direct me somewhere dodgy, or I'd kick his arse! He might have been old but he could have quite easily had me turned over. We shook on it and said he was very happy with our business arrangement, so off we went.

Along the way we started to make small talk and I discovered him to be a very honest, very witty old man living on the streets – someone's father, someone's former husband, someone's older brother coming from a typically big family in the divided south of the great US of A. I do say that with some sarcasm because of the way these people were treated, but that's politics and I'm staying out of it. Anyway, I'd found myself a drinking buddy and was going to buy him a drink in the first bar we came across, which was right ahead of us. To my shock I was really surprised to see the, lets say fear, on his face once I invited him in with me. This was crazy I thought, so it made me even more determined to buy him that drink despite what people might have said to him just because of his colour or appearance – which I might add was still respectable considering his circumstances.

Even in the face of possible aggravation he still kept his dignity and friendly manner, which I really respected him for – in fact I thought if anyone was going to kick off it was me, but he just stood there and took it, and nudged me as if to say, 'Keep it cool I've heard it all before.' I mean it wasn't verbal abuse, it was more the looks and whisperings that I could see going on y'know. It was a real eye-opener for me which convinced me to take Edmund with me to the next bar then another, and another, having some good laughs along the way. We even paid a visit to a 'titty bar' which he really appreciated and enjoyed – not to say that he's never been in one before, but just to see him having a good time was fulfilling enough for me. Me and my mate Ed had a fantastic night – we laughed and drank like old buddies do y'know. As the night drew to a close and the street lights had finished their shift, to be replaced by God's sunlight, we headed off to the casino for a buffet breakfast.

Those buffet breakfast are a real treat, everything you can think of is there – I love them. And so did Edmund by the look at the size of his portions - for a skinny guy, boy, could he eat!

Our business deal came to an end outside as we shook on the deal and I paid him in full, plus a few more dollars to carry on his weekend with. The night was a special night for me – two strangers meeting, forming a friendship, if only for the night, and having a guys' night out despite what colour we were, or our social differences or backgrounds. And I genuinely think that Ed also enjoyed the night, despite the fact I was returning to my 5-Star address compared to his accustomed bed for the night, whether it be cardboard or a mattress. I did feel sorry for the guy, but I hope I brought a smile to his face, for a couple of hours anyway. I often think of him now and then, and chuckle to myself whenever I read this chapter of the laughs we had. I doubt whether he would have lasted much longer living on those mean streets – this story goes back nearly 20 years so he's probably dead now, God bless him.

Ed, you're the man, this chapter's for you buddy!

Footnote
While me and Ed were moving from bar to bar a police car pulled up along side me. 'Shit,' I thought, 'Whats going on 'ere?' The officer got out of his car to approach me but as he got closer to me he held out his hand and give me a warm handshake!

He went on to say that he heard my English accent and wanted to take the time to say 'hello' and to say 'thank you' for England's support in standing with America after September 11th events. I was gobsmacked as the burly guy give me a big bear hug then made friendly talk with me before he jumped back into his car then drove off. It was a touching moment and it fitted in perfectly in what was a perfect night out. It was very surreal though.

Twenty-Three
Closing Thoughts

It's been very pleasing for me to sit down and actually put some of my experiences down on paper. During the whole time it's taken me I've had no problems sacrificing nights down at the pub or a day in the sun to have my stories completed. If you'd 'ave said to me when I was younger and in my teens that I'd be writing a book I would 'ave laughed out loudly but here I am 46 years old, feeling really chuffed with myself for doing so.

The book itself only really covers a small amount of the fun I've had travelling about and the amount of friends I've made along the way means it's almost impossible to remember them all. But the ones I do remember I have great affection for, each and every one of them. Without them my photos and book means nothing. So I'd like to say a huge 'Thank You' to them all, wherever they are — Cheers guys.

While I was in the midst of writing I would often giggle away to myself as my stories unfolded and the memories came flooding back, which for me was the whole purpose of putting my photo albums together and now this, my book. One of the things that scares me about getting old is losing all these memories. The thought of my children, grandchildren or Harry and Jamie coming to me and asking me about them and a frail old man not being able to tell them what they want to hear, really is upsetting. Or even telling people of my experiences and not having anything to back it up with. There's nothing worse than a bullshitter who can't back it up. Well now I can feel pleased with myself in knowing that they can look at my albums then read the book. If they can read my adventures and marvel at my pictures and then say to themselves 'Wow he's had a good entertaining life hasn't he?' then the life I set out to have has been accomplished, shared and appreciated by others.

I've settled down now and share a flat with my soul mate and longtime girlfriend Trudy of six years and have worked for a successful internet company that sells adult toys called Lovehoney for about six years now. My life is good and I feel very fortunate to have experienced and enjoyed the travelling lifestyle. I'd be lying if I didn't say that from time to time I look through my albums and reminiscence about my adventures but I'm happy to close them and let them collect dust and be there for when Harry and Jamie want to come over and browse through them.

On a different note, away from travelling, I'm now a successful Level Two Amateur Boxing coach for Bath City Boxing Club. My next goal I've set for myself is to run a successful boxing club. I'd love to be able to bring young kids along and be a mentor for them, teaching them discipline and respect, as well as being able to look after themselves. It didn't do me any harm!

I love what I do and it brings stability in my life. I also love to write, it's a passion of mine that I discovered while I was attending a Media and Journalism course just before I got married. I only wish I could conjure up exquisite words like that of a Brian Blessed or a Stephen Fry, but I'm happy with what I put down – it works for me.

During the Rugby League season I write my own page for the match day programme of my beloved St Helens Rugby League Club. Having my own page came as bit of a shock to me when I received the email from the clubs media manager after I sent him some samples of what I've written in the past, and a template of the idea I had in mind. Along with my comeback fight I think it's one of my greatest achievements, which I hope to continue with for as long as they'll have me. My name will always be there in print and be associated with the club.

I mentioned in an earlier chapter that the world is a huge place so go out and see it, well I did and nowadays when it comes to mine and Trudy's holidays we like nothing better than staying in the UK and going to places like Cornwall and Devon. 'Been there, seen it, done it, bought the T-shirt' is the common phrase, and we love nothing better than to take in the beautiful coastal scenery of good old Blighty. As beautiful as the world may be you can't beat home.

I would like to end on a thankful note.

During your lifetime so many people contribute to your life it makes it impossible to remember them and thank them all. Some have moved away and lost touch, others have sadly passed on. That's how life is but it's your family who you can always count on and will always be there for you. So, once again, I would like to thank my mum Barbara, my dad Ray and my sister Allison for being there for me whenever I came home and needed a bed, some food and my washing done.

Ian for being the best brother-in-law and getting me hooked on Saints, and my girlfriend Trudy who whilst I was spending lots of time away at my desk completing what I'd started would pop her head round the door asking me if I wanted a cuppa tea. Trudy was also responsible for putting me in touch with Wendy Cooper of Biographies & Memoirs from an ad she noticed in our neighbourhood magazine, so thank you baby and thank you Wendy.

Finally, and not forgotten, Harry and Jamie. My love for them two boys inspired me to write this book. Enjoy it boys and I hope I'll always be your hero.

Love to you all.